# LIFE
# DESIGN
### FOR
# WOMEN

# LIFE
# DESIGN
## FOR
# WOMEN

Conscious Living as a Force
for Positive Change

## ARIANE BURGESS

FINDHORN PRESS

Findhorn Press
One Park Street
Rochester, Vermont 05767
www.findhornpress.com

Text stock is SFI certified

Findhorn Press is a division of Inner Traditions International

**Disclaimer**
The information in this book is given in good faith and intended for information only. Neither author nor publisher can be held liable by any person for any loss or damage whatsoever which may arise from the use of this book or any of the information therein.

A CIP record for this title is available from the Library of Congress

ISBN 978-1-62055-915-4 (print)
ISBN 978-1-62055-916-1 (ebook)

Printed and bound in the United States by Lake Book Manufacturing, Inc. The text stock is SFI certified. The Sustainable Forestry Initiative® program promotes sustainable forest management.

10 9 8 7 6 5 4 3 2 1

Edited by Nicky Leach
Line drawings by Ariane Burgess
Word Cloud drawings by Eddy Coodee
Cover illustrations by Vectorstock (white flower) and Ariane Burgess
Text design and layout by Damian Keenan
This book was typeset in Adobe Garamond Pro, Calluna Sans and Museo with Bernhard Modern Std used as a display typeface.

To send correspondence to the author of this book, mail a first-class letter to the author c/o Inner Traditions • Bear & Company, One Park Street, Rochester, VT 05767, USA, and we will forward the communication, or contact the author directly at **arianeburgess.com**

# Contents

# Introduction

In 2000, I collaborated on a campaign aimed at preventing over a hundred New York City community gardens from being destroyed. At the height of the campaign, just as I was planning to email invitations to an outreach and fund-raising event, a proactive friend and environmentalist from the community garden movement questioned me about using the word "invitation." He said that people shouldn't need an invitation to do something good for the planet. They should just come.

He's right in some ways. No one needs an invitation to do something good for the planet, to join a movement, and I too used to think people should be rushing to participate in ensuring a living future for all life. However, as a result of my years of being active in people and planet care work, doing what I could to live in ways that might contribute to a future for the next generations of humans and all other species on Earth, I have come to feel that issuing an invitation is necessary. Yes, some people will come to events of their own volition—and at the time of writing, more do so everyday—but not enough, and not fast enough.

Whether it's in the hustle and bustle of New York City or the peace and quiet of the Findhorn ecovillage in Scotland, it's more often than not the same handful of people who step up and lean in to do what it takes to contribute to a thriving future. If we're really going to make that future possible, more people need to join in. I'm glad you're here, and I hope you will join us. This book, *Life Design for Women*, is an invitation to join the movement to act for life on Earth through "regenerative living and leading."

We are living with a confluence of crisis points that affect us all. We may think we can hole up in our homes and get on with our lives, keeping everything that is unpleasant from affecting or harming us. It is inevitable, however, that in some way or other, the crisis will arrive at our doorstep.

The impact of the 2008 financial crisis was systemic, so even if you didn't take out a faulty loan, you might have been personally affected by it, perhaps losing your home, your job, or your retirement fund. I have a friend who retired from teaching in public school in 2006. She had worked all her life and paid into her pension plan, but when the financial crisis hit, she lost half of her retirement fund. The economic system is broken. It only works for a few, usually those who already have some kind of privilege to begin with. It doesn't work for the majority of people on the planet—and it's not working for the planet, either.

Our health is also being affected. More and more people are feeling socially isolated and suffering from mental health challenges such as anxiety and depression. While there are tremendous advances in the health sector, well-funded research and innovation still haven't stopped the advance of cancer. The majority of the population in most Western countries is over 55, and the health and care systems are stretched thin, as more people find themselves living with conditions such as dementia and diabetes.

At long last, we are beginning to acknowledge that our material and financial success is the cause of environmental collapse, as evidenced by the speed with which species are dying out, our discovery that microplastics can now be found in the deepest parts of Earth's oceans, and learning that industrial-scale farming used to grow our food is polluting our waterways and depleting soil fertility.

The environmental catastrophe that is finally capturing our attention is climate change, which is happening so fast that even scientists on the Intergovernmental Panel on Climate Change (IPCC) can't keep up with all of the events pushing up global temperatures—something that should alarm us all.

The climate change we are currently experiencing is mainly caused by human industrial activities. These activities emit greenhouse gases that cause Earth's overall temperature to rise. A rise in temperature of only a few degrees has led to environmental and human catastrophe. Villages, towns, and cities all over the world are being devastated by floods, hurricanes, tornadoes, landslides, and fires, all of which can be linked to changes in Earth's temperature. In some areas, whole villages or regional populations are being displaced from their homes and land. This adds to the refugee crisis, as people migrate from their homelands in the hope of finding a place to live.

These are just a few of the distressing issues we face. I'm sure you can come up with others. You may have been personally impacted. It's a lot to take in. No wonder many people have been turning away from it rather than responding. It's so overwhelming that it's hard to know where to begin. What would be a useful and meaningful response?

While life on Earth as we know it is being decimated through human activities, the planet will continue to evolve in some form long after we're gone. Right now, what is happening is that we humans are busy destroying the delicately balanced living environment that makes life, including human life, possible. Earth is a unique, rare habitat in which we thrive, along with all the plants and animals. There is no other known planet in our solar system so perfectly set up for human life. It is we humans who need to be saved. We need to be saved from ourselves, so that future generations of life on Earth have a chance to live. Rather than turning our backs and saying that it's not our problem, the fact that these crises exist demonstrates that we are all being asked to engage in radical and mutually beneficial change.

Fortunately, people *are* engaging, particularly with the reality of the long-term impact of rising temperatures on the planet.

In 2018, Swedish school student Greta Thunberg staged the first school strike for the climate. She skipped school and stood outside the Swedish parliament building, demanding that the Swedish government honor its commitment to the United Nations 2015 Paris Agreement and take action to reduce carbon emissions. Her actions catalyzed the international #ClimateStrike movement, which has seen thousands of school students all around the world walk out of school on Friday mornings, demanding that their governments take rapid action to reduce the emissions of greenhouse gases.

"I want you to panic, and I want you to feel the fear I feel every day," Greta told the global elite who were attending their annual World Economic Forum in Davos, Switzerland in January 2019.

Another movement that surged to prominence in the UK in 2018 and went global is Extinction Rebellion, or XR. As part of Extinction Rebellion, people of all ages around the world are using creative forms of protest, including nonviolent civil disobedience, to bring attention to the planetary ecocide that is currently occurring. They are so concerned about what's happening to the planet that they're willing to be arrested as a way to gain media attention and make more of us aware of the need to take action.

In April 2019, more than one thousand people were arrested in London over several weeks of ongoing nonviolent civil disobedience. The activists' work put climate change at the top of the media agenda every day. Finally, people were engaging with the issue. Even an early morning money program on BBC radio had climate change as its primary topic every day that week.

Regenerative Living and Leading, and the Life Design process described in this book, is not about getting arrested or going on strike. It is about identifying the ways in which your lifestyle perpetuates degenerative planetary destruction and transforming it through strategic, radical changes to a lifestyle in which you make a life-affirming, regenerative contribution through your daily choices and actions. Getting arrested or going on strike may emerge as an action you will take as a result of your personal Life Design process, but you can also participate powerfully from the comfort of your own home.

I have heard women say, "I don't know where to begin."

Life Design for Women is a response to this confusion. We begin with ourselves; we then work together to make changes on a local and community level and campaign at the national level, using the power of our government to introduce legislation requiring that corporations rapidly transition to regenerative, life-supporting practices in their business models.

If you just want to focus on the positive, bright side of life, this book is not for you. There will be a bright side, certainly, but before you get there, you will have to be willing to dig deep, look at the ugly parts of your life, transform those parts you've pushed away, and integrate what you discover into a way of living you consciously choose.

I originally conceived of the Life Design process as an annual goal-setting workbook. I wanted to provide women with a goal-setting structure in which they could define what success looked like to them and include the planet in those goals. It became clear, though, that I needed to provide more context, including my belief that we need to change the way we set our goals, and also to clarify the design process. *Life Design for Women* is what emerged.

I wrote for my peers: women in their forties into their sixties, who are at a stage in their life in which they have time to reflect and chart a more meaningful course. For these women, this time has opened up perhaps because they are established in their career, they have a stable home life, or their children (if they had them) are grown to a point that they are no longer relying on Mom. For many women in this age range, it's also the time when we go through menopause, so the energy our bodies used to maintain the monthly cycle of activating an egg for fertilization can now be consciously directed in other creative ways.

During the writing process, however, I met younger women who, when they heard what I was doing, said: "I want to read that!" If you are reading this book and haven't yet made decisions about starting a family, you will find that there are a few things missing, mainly the part about having children and being a mother. The Life Design process will still be of value to you, and by encouraging you to explore other areas of your life deeply, may usefully contribute to your decisions about having children and motherhood.

My intention with the Life Design process is not to give you the answers; it's to encourage you to think, reflect, and explore your way into your life, for yourself. Life Design simply gives prompts and signposts for directions you might take.

This is an invitation to embark on the journey of a lifetime—a journey in conscious personal transformation for the sake of all life on Earth, a journey in which you design your life, design *for* life, and design *with* Life.

## The Journey

When embarking on any journey, it is helpful to know a bit about the path you'll be walking. Your unique details will emerge as you explore your life. This book is organized in a particular order; however, if there's an area of your life you feel drawn to work on, start there. Before you enter the Life Design process in Part 3, the following sections provide a context for you to consider as you design change into your life.

**PART 1, "IN THE BEGINNING,"** is essential reading and foundational to the Life Design process. It's the framing that makes *Life Design for Women* truly a design for all life. Without understanding that there's a dominant worldview that perpetuates a default way of living and meeting our needs and that dictates to us what we should value, we might as well be working with a business-as-usual process. In this part, I also highlight a few reasons as to why now is the time for women to step forward and lead, and I provide some useful models we can work with as we embark on the process of deep adaptation.

**IN PART 2, "GATHERING TOOLS,"** I explore the purpose of Life Design and introduce you to the Life Design process of **OREDA** – Observe, Reflect, Envision, Define, and Act. I also offer 10 tools in Chapter 7 to assist you on your path. They include things to be aware of or attitudes you might want to adopt as well as two tools you will use in the designing process. Adopting just one of them will have a beneficial impact.

**PART 3, "LIFE DESIGN: DIVING INTO YOUR DOMAINS,"** is the heart of the book, where, using **OREDA**, you explore your life and identify the life-affirming changes you want to make.

At the end of the book, you'll find three powerful exercises in Resources and a bibliography listing books, websites, and videos to support your Life Design process and ongoing learning.

# 1

## *In the Beginning*

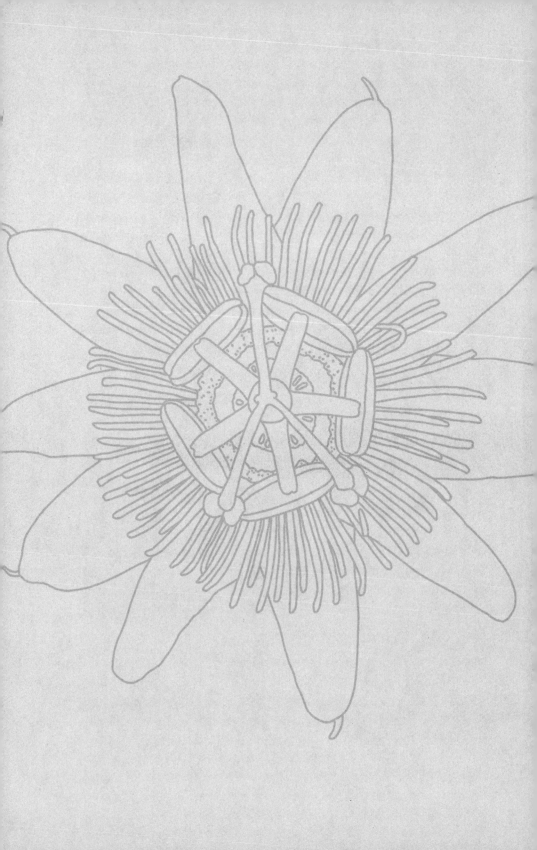

# CHAPTER 1

# Context Matters

Let's begin with our context. If we're going to make changes in our lives, it's important for us to recognize the context we live in. We need to take a broader view. There are reasons it's difficult to make changes, and it's not all to do with having the motivation or not. Some of it has to do with the context we live in.

Our human-designed systems, which are intended to meet our needs and wants for living, are in conflict with the way nature needs to operate to provide our fundamental life-support systems. Our wasteful lifestyles are destroying nature's systems. We can make personal and individual life-benefitting decisions in our behavior, but they can be difficult to maintain because the context we're living in is set up in a way that perpetuates the destruction of nature. An underlying worldview that plays a role in our constantly defaulting to this destructive behavior is the assumption that the only way for humans to prosper is through economic growth.

A worldview is a particular human-formed philosophy or way of seeing the world. Our worldviews fuel our values, which are in turn made visible through the choices we make, the actions we take, and the events in which we engage or are exposed to. Our worldviews shape the physical world around us, and they shape us. In a single day, we are exposed to a wide range of worldviews, and we may participate, consciously or unconsciously, in perpetuating and cultivating one or more of them. Worldviews are formed through our experiences with our immediate environment, from which our traditions, ways of doing things, belief systems, and language developed. There are innumerable worldviews in the world, making up the rich tapestry of cultures we see around us today.

What's challenging about worldviews is that we grow up within them, so it's hard to understand that we are living within a specific worldview and that there are other ways to live. Like goldfish swimming in a fish bowl, we are unaware of the water and the bowl, as we don't have any other experience to compare our current experience with. We first encounter worldviews through our parents and family, and the society we grow up in, our school and community groups, including religious ones, and the media. Because everyone around us lives in this same way, the worldview remains unseen and unquestioned.

Since the end of the Second World War, the economic growth worldview has spread globally and has eclipsed other local worldviews that inform local, traditional cultures. In this worldview, the way national wealth is measured, how we are doing as a country, is measured by gross domestic product, or GDP. GDP is the amount of goods and services that are sold over a period of time, quarterly or annually for example. From this perspective, the more goods and services are sold, the better off we are. GDP as an indicator doesn't count the impact that producing the goods or providing the services has on the environment or the humans involved. Missing from this indicator is the well-being of the people and the planet.

This worldview is limited to only valuing life in economic terms, conflating true wealth with material and financial wealth. It assumes that once we have all our material and financial needs met, we will have well-being and will be happy. There is more to this, however, than having money and things. Yes, both are important, but not at the expense of essentials for well-being, like having clean air to breathe and fresh water to drink, time to enjoy being with our loved ones or to develop new skills.

## The Benefits of the Economic Growth Worldview

People living in countries like the United States of America, Canada, Australia and in Europe have enjoyed the results of this worldview for decades: enhanced material wealth and quality of life. Now, in other parts of the world, as developing countries also embrace this economic worldview as well, the people living there begin to experience the benefits of it.

We have the convenience of turning on the tap for a constant supply of fresh water rather than having to walk miles to the nearest well and then carry a heavy water pitcher home on our heads. As the sun sets, with the flick of a switch our rooms are bathed in electric light, and without a second thought we are able to use all our gadgets, computers, hair dryers, and toasters. Our homes are built to provide good shelter, and we can regulate the temperature, prepare and eat food, and sleep comfortably and securely.

We can own or rent transport, a car or three, and there are private and public transport companies that provide bus, train, and airplane travel services. We have leisure time for self-discovery and relaxation. In some countries, when we pay taxes, in return we have access to education, health-care, and our waste is collected and disposed of in a way that we don't even have to see, let alone wade through it. Generally, our health has improved, with longer life expectancy supported by surgery and medicines.

While, in part, the proponents of the economic growth worldview had the noble intention of improving the quality of life for people, what they did not consider was the impact on the natural environment. We are now operating within a worldview that economic thinkers conceived and developed at a time when there was no understanding that we live on a finite planet, and that nature and time have a deep, long-standing relationship, which brought about the abundance our ancestors once experienced.

This worldview saw the clean air, fresh water, abundantly fertile soils, vast mineral and precious metal deposits, and old forests as endless resources that could be used for material and financial gain without the need to restore or replenish them. There was no awareness of the detrimental impact the rapacious practice of continually taking from Earth's natural systems, without giving back, would have. By the time people did start to recognize the problems involved, this worldview had already taken hold, and so many people were benefiting from it that the long-term environmental impacts were overlooked, and often knowingly denied.

In this worldview, maximum financial profit is the primary goal. In order to maximize profit, a company designs its production processes in such a way that natural resources, whether it is the mountain top blown off for the extraction of coal or the river that is polluted by toxic waste, are seen as externalities. Externalities are not included in the cost of bringing the item to market, and can be either positive or negative. A company takes no responsibility for these externalities, especially when they are negative. The negative impact of externalities is borne by nature and by people living in poor neighborhoods or in the world's developing countries, where they live in a polluted environment or work in life-threatening conditions.

In the case of nature, if companies are chasing financial profit while disregarding the negative impact of the externalities, their production process threatens to destroy the delicately balanced conditions that make life on Earth possible.

A convenient story included in this worldview—one that aids the shirking of responsibility for what happens as a consequence of globalized, industrial production—is that nature is inanimate, a machine from which we can extract the parts with no consequence. This perspective makes it possible to blow the tops off mountains in West Virginia to extract coal, cut down the Amazon rainforest at the rate of a football pitch per second for timber, and confine millions of cows in Concentrated Animal Feeding Operations (CAFOs), feeding them corn, a grain that their bodies cannot naturally digest, to fatten them up quickly for market.

While the system for creating wealth has improved life for many of us, looked at closely you can see that it also has the effect of creating astounding wealth for a small group of people, while many people in the world live in poverty and have become increasingly vulnerable to losing their land and homes due to natural disasters.

Proponents of this worldview use powerful and continuous messages to propel us consciously and unconsciously into perpetuating it. We participate in this unraveling process—either through regularly consuming products and services we often don't really need or pursuing extreme financial and material wealth in a desperate attempt to create security and safety for ourselves and our family. The message we get is that we have to perpetuate economic growth and shop till we drop in order to live, in order to feel safe.

What is hidden from us is the fact that as we keep consuming and pursuing material and financial wealth in these ways, we destroy all forms of life, and when that happens, we've effectively destroyed ourselves. This worldview is way past its sell-by date. We urgently need to throw it out.

We are in a struggle for survival in which the wealth-creating worldview of economic growth, and the actions that stem from it, is pitted against the fact that we need the wealth nature provides for all life on Earth. What is becoming clear is that it is not possible to have material and financial wealth without causing life-threatening damage to the planet and to other people. We can no longer accept that the life-diminishing impacts on the planet and on people working for companies are considered externalities.

## Regenerative Worldview

We need a new worldview that recognizes the preciousness of nature and the worth of all people. We need a worldview that puts the design of how we create financial and material wealth within the boundaries of our finite planet. This worldview needs to make the regeneration and stewardship of nature's life support systems integral to all human ways of living. It needs to value forests and mountains, wildcats and elephants, and women, children, and men—not as resources or workers used to create financial and material wealth for the few but for their own intrinsic worth.

For decades, we have been talking about and trying to work with the idea of meeting human needs in a way that also sustains Earth's natural systems. Collectively, we haven't done a very good job of this. The concept of economic growth has continued to drive our actions and as a result many of nature's systems have collapsed or are collapsing to the point that there are no longer any well-functioning systems to sustain or maintain. We urgently need to evolve our approach and begin immediately designing our lives in a way that supports nature to regenerate.

As Life Designers, if we set our life goals within the same economic growth worldview, we continue to participate in perpetuating the destruction, which is why we need to look deeply into our lives to explore how this economic worldview shapes us and decide whether it works for us or not. We need to look for and create other worldviews that have a broader, more life-sustaining perspective of wealth, ones that include regeneration at the core, and we can start that process with ourselves.

Some environmentalists are uncomfortable with laying the responsibility of what's happening to the planet at the feet of individuals. It should be the responsibility of the people who created the system, or for policy makers and politicians to put legislation in place that curtails profit-driven corporations from continuing their life-destroying way of doing business.

I think it's both. We need personal change as well as systemic change. As individuals, we are all active participants in the system . . . in many different systems. If we change ourselves, the system will change. If we all make changes that support nature's regeneration, even if we don't personally know the other people who are making similar changes, our changes will add up and have a collective impact. Simultaneously, for those of us fortunate enough to live in some form of democracy, we need to engage our political voice and demand legislation that can have a far-reaching impact on business practices that our personal changes can't affect.

We need to approach the intertwined crises from multiple directions.

Joanna Macy, deep ecologist and systems thinker, points out that we are at a decision point. We can continue the current path of "business as usual" and along with it, the Great Unraveling, or we can make a conscious choice to turn things around and create the Great Turning. In the Great Turning, there are three ways we can actively participate: we can take actions in defense of life on Earth, actions that transform how we live, and actions that transform our worldview and values. As Life Designers, we are working on all three fronts of the Great Turning.

# CHAPTER 2

# Models in Support of a Regenerative Approach

Fortunately, we are not alone; some people have been seeking ways to support life on Earth for a long time and are coming up with ways of thinking, frameworks, and models that will help us navigate in this pioneering and uncharted territory.

Below, I highlight a few of these. They may not all seem relevant to your life and Life Design process, and some of them have yet to embrace ideas of regeneration, but as we work on personal transformation and developing a new collective worldview, it is essential that we understand the context within which we are designing and start to gather tools that can help us act for life.

## Ecological Literacy

A foundational place to begin is to develop our ecological literacy, or eco-literacy as it is often referred to. Ecological literacy is the understanding of how natural systems function to make life on Earth possible and to apply this to creating regenerative human settlements—villages or towns, for example.

Educator David Orr and physicist Fritjof Capra developed the ideas behind eco-literacy in the 1990s, drawing inspiration from their observations of nature. In the book *The Systems View of Life*, co-authored by Capra and Pier Luigi Luisi, they write about the need for us to learn "the fundamental facts of life—that one species' waste is another species' food; that matter cycles continually through the web of life; that the energy driving the ecological cycles flows from the sun; that diversity assures resilience; that life, from its beginning more than 3 billion years ago, did not take over the planet by combat but by networking."

I encourage you to explore further these fundamental facts of life so your understanding becomes second nature to you. A good place to begin is by simply observing what occurs in nature.

## Sustainable Development Goals

In 2015, the United Nations (UN) published the report *Transforming Our World: the 2030 Agenda for Sustainable Development.* This document includes 17 Sustainable Development Goals (SDGs), the purpose of which is to provide internationally recognized goals for development. While I believe we have long passed the option for sustainability and need to move to a regenerative approach—designing ways to meet our human needs while actively supporting nature to regenerate—the UN's SDGs provide valuable directions for UN member countries to work toward in terms of planning and policy setting. As you read the goals you could replace the word sustainable with regenerative.

What is essential to understand about the UN and the SDGs is that they have emerged out of the economic growth worldview, so while they are useful goals, they don't go far enough. There is also the tension between the developed and the developing countries of the world. Quite rightly, people living in developing countries want to have the same economic wealth benefits as those of us in developed countries, and they want to see the developed countries pay for the damage they've done. The problem is that the planet cannot even sustain the lifestyle of those of us living in the developed world.

The Sustainable Development Goals are:

**GOAL 1**    End poverty in all its forms everywhere.

**GOAL 2**    End hunger, achieve food security and improved nutrition, and promote sustainable agriculture.

**GOAL 3**    Ensure healthy lives and promote well-being for all at all ages.

**GOAL 4**    Ensure inclusive and equitable quality education and promote lifelong learning opportunities for all.

**GOAL 5**    Achieve gender equality and empower all women and girls.

**GOAL 6**    Ensure availability and sustainable management of water and sanitation for all.

**GOAL 7**    Ensure access to affordable, reliable, sustainable, and modern energy for all.

**GOAL 8**    Promote sustained, inclusive, and sustainable economic growth, full and productive employment, and decent work for all.

**GOAL 9**    Build resilient infrastructure, promote inclusive and sustainable industrialization, and foster innovation.

**GOAL 10**   Reduce inequality within and among countries.

**GOAL 11**  Make cities and human settlements inclusive, safe, resilient, and sustainable.

**GOAL 12**  Ensure sustainable consumption and production patterns.

**GOAL 13**  Make urgent action to combat climate change and its impacts.

**GOAL 14**  Conserve and sustainably use the oceans, seas, and marine resources for sustainable development.

**GOAL 15**  Protect, restore, and promote sustainable use of terrestrial ecosystems, sustainably manage forests, combat desertification, and halt and reverse land degradation and halt biodiversity loss.

**GOAL 16**  Promote peaceful and inclusive societies for sustainable development, provide access to justice for all and build effective, accountable, and inclusive institutions at all levels.

**GOAL 17**  Strengthen the means of implementation, and revitalize the global partnership for sustainable development.

## Planetary Boundaries

The concept of Planetary Boundaries offers a model that can help us understand the parameters within which we need to live to support nature. Pioneering scientists Johan Rockström from the Stockholm Resilience Centre and Will Steffen from the Australian National University identified "nine processes that regulate the stability and resilience of the Earth system." These processes are based on Earth System Science (ESS), specifically the interactions among Earth's "spheres"—atmosphere, hydrosphere, cryosphere, geosphere, pedosphere, biosphere, and magnetosphere. Who knew there were so many spheres?

Using scientific analysis, they defined boundaries for each of the processes that offer what Rockström calls a "safe operating space" within which human activity needs to stay if we want to ensure nature's life-support systems continue to function into the future.

The nine planetary boundaries are quantified by specific measurements within which we need to operate, including: biogeochemical levels of nitrogen and phosphorus imposed through human activity, the level of ocean acidification, the amount of land turned over to growing crops, the amount of fresh water available for consumption globally, the concentration of ozone in our stratosphere, the concentration of airborne particulate matter in our atmosphere, and the concentration of combined chemical pollution including toxic substances, plastics, heavy metals, and endocrine disruptors.

Planetary Boundaries Model (Rockström and Steffen)

Two planetary boundaries you likely have heard of are climatic warming and loss of biodiversity, which are in the news because we have already overshot the planetary boundary for each of them. As far as a safe operating space for the climate goes, we are on track to exceed the 1.5 degrees Celsius limit set by the Paris Agreement in 2015, while in the case of the loss of biodiversity, we have entered what American biologist E. O. Wilson calls the Sixth Great Extinction.

These proposed nine boundaries have been robustly debated and critiqued by other scientists. Some say having a boundary is dangerous because we may then think we can go right up to the boundary level. Others support the boundaries, as they give policymakers tools to work with.

Planetary boundaries give us guidelines for ways to live within our natural environment, but what about our social systems?

## Doughnut Economics

While working at Oxfam, economist Kate Raworth synthesized the SDGs into what she calls the Social Foundations. She identified them as:

- food
- water
- health
- energy
- networks
- housing

- gender equality
- social equity
- political voice
- peace and justice
- income and work
- education

She then put a hole in the center of the planetary boundary model and inserted the 12 social foundations to create what she calls Doughnut Economics, because, visually, the model looks like a doughnut.

The inner ring describes the bottom limit of the social foundations, and the outer ring is the planetary boundaries. It is a powerful visual, as it shows clearly how we are failing globally to ensure that everyone has basic social foundations and that we are pushing to the edge of, and in some cases beyond, the planetary boundaries. The ring of the doughnut shows us the parameters within which our economics need to operate in order for life on Earth to survive the 21st century and beyond.

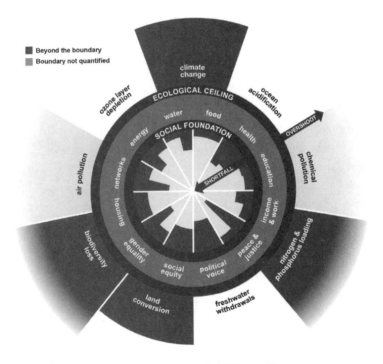

Doughnut Economics Model (Raworth)

The model gives us our safe operating framework, but how do we bring it to life? We need to start by reconciling our relationship with nature and allowing ourselves to have experiences that remind us that nature is alive and made up of millions of interdependent forms of life cooperating to create a delicately balanced biosphere. Then we need to find embodied ways of recognizing that we are in fact part of nature and through this, we need to start finding our regenerative contribution and place in the whole.

We need to delve into our lives and unpick the assumptions we live with about what constitutes financial and material wealth and find out what true wealth—true well-being—means for us. We need to explore what drives us to seek security and safety. Through this strategic work, we can start to inhabit our Sovereign Self, the self that has the agency and power to participate in the course correction that's badly needed.

## Regenerative Enterprise

In their book *Regenerative Enterprise: Optimizing for Multi-Capital Abundance*, authors Ethan Roland and Gregory Landua of Regenerative Enterprise Institute put forward what they call the Eight Forms of Capital. This model proposes a different approach to business, one that sees wealth creation beyond financial and material capital. They draw on existing models that acknowledge social and natural capital but also include living, experiential, intellectual, spiritual, and cultural capital.

- Living capital
- Social capital
- Experiential capital
- Intellectual capital
- Financial capital
- Material capital
- Spiritual capital
- Cultural capital

In the economic growth business model, corporations use social, experiential, and intellectual capital to turn living capital into financial and material capital, while spiritual and cultural capital are seen as externalities and most often destroyed. Roland and Landua propose that corporations adopt a regenerative approach to manufacturing their goods and providing services that creatively accommodates all eight capitals into their business model.

In our personal lives, these Eight Forms of Capital are a useful measurement of whether we have a good balance of capitals.

CHAPTER 3

# Women Are the Future

As a result of our biological ability to give birth—and for some, the longing to have children—women embody the future. We can give, and have literally given, birth to the future by birthing the next generation. Those of us who have had children have created a connection to the future, carried it in our bodies for nine months, and birthed it as our children, and in time, their children. The act of having children is a declaration of the desire for humanity to continue existing.

Women have yet to fully play an equivalent role in shaping life on Earth. The majority of human systems set up to meet our needs and create wealth have been designed by men—specifically, white men who have a particular life experience and perspective. For women to have equivalence with men, we need to change the worldview—one that isn't working for 99 percent of the population of this planet, or for nature and the millions of species of animals and plants.

At a time when humanity has so much to lose, women have nothing to lose and much to gain by strategically, authentically, and urgently responding to the overshoot crisis of the planetary boundaries and the gaping cracks in our collective social foundations. As a result of the courageous pioneering work of women who lived and struggled for equivalence in the past, the opportunities for us now to have a say in how things are done is increasing, and yet we still have a long way to go.

These human-designed systems were conceived at a time when we didn't understand that we need to live within a safe operating space that ensures that nature's life-support systems can function. We have known for decades that it is impossible to have a wealth-creating system solely focused on financial and material gain without causing suffering to others, not to mention, dire consequences for the future of life on Earth. And yet, we carry on.

Women are increasingly looking for ways to live that cause less pain and suffering in the world and to the planet. I know this from talking with them. I organize and teach Regenerative Design courses, providing participants with ideas, tools, and skills for living a more sustainable, regenerative life, and 80 percent of the course participants are women. When I ask them why they come, they share their concerns about what is happening around them, and that they are worried about the future of life on Earth. They want to learn ways to change the way they live and be able to meaningfully influence and contribute to how that is being done in their families and communities. They want to achieve a more life-affirming outcome.

Women who live in countries that have been operating within the Western economic worldview for decades recognize they have benefitted from the material advances that stem from this worldview. They are also aware that there is no such thing as an externality, and that the economic model creates intractable problems for people and the planet. Women are actively looking for new ways of doing things.

The Dalai Lama caused quite a stir at the 2009 Peace Summit in Vancouver. He said that "the world would be saved by Western women." His statement received a range of responses, but many women found it empowering, and it catalyzed women-focused initiatives.

The Dalai Lama specifically said that Western women are the ones to do the saving. From my perspective, the changes humans need to make will happen through everyone's conscious effort. Perhaps he singled Western women out because less of us are living in survival mode; we have our basic needs for clean air, water, food, and housing met. Unlike women in other parts of the world, women who live in developed countries, the countries that benefitted from colonialism—Europe, North America, Australia, and New Zealand—hold a tremendous amount of privilege and power, and using this, we can have a huge positive impact. The privilege and power we possess stems from our education, economic stability, and increasing political voice. If we wield this power wisely, we could individually and collectively have an impact that brings back the planet and all life on Earth from the brink of extinction.

We have reasons to change the current story of how human needs are met. The economic growth worldview contains vestiges of a narrative that women are inferior to men. While women make up 50 percent of the world's population, and well above that figure in the United States and Europe, we still live in a world that serves men first. In recent years, this has expressed itself through the simple fact that women are paid less than men for doing equivalent work and only a tiny percentage of women are company directors. We continue to face sexual harassment in the workplace and violence in our own homes, which have been raised to a new level of awareness and action by the #MeToo movement.

While education can offer opportunities for women, it is still the case that girls and boys are encouraged in different ways at school. According to 2008 data from the National Science Foundation, only 20 percent of engineering graduates in the United States were women, and a 2013 review by the American Association of University Women showed that only 26 percent of computer professionals were women. Since Artificial Intelligence (AI) will dramatically shape our future, it is essential that women are involved in how it is designed.

The author of *The Gendered Brain: The New Neuroscience that Shatters the Myth of the Female Brain*, Gina Rippon, Professor of Cognitive Neuroimaging at Aston University in the United Kingdom, tells of her experience growing up as a twin. She was academically bright, scoring top in the country to gain a scholarship to a grammar school, yet her parents sent her to a non-academic Catholic convent. Her brother, who had no interest in academics and went on to become an artist, was sent to an academic Catholic boarding school. This was the inciting circumstance that propelled Professor Rippon to pursue her research, which showed that the brain, the way human intelligence is so often measured, is no different in a man or a woman.

While women are becoming increasingly visible in politics across the world, it is still the exception. Until recently, the majority of these politicians participated in upholding the old and limited vision for the world: that wealth is only based on financial and material capital. A well-considered plan of how we collectively thrive into the future is needed, and to do that we need legislation that is created through a diversity of experience and perspectives.

Women have increased economic spending power today, and companies are very much aware of this and direct a considerable amount of their marketing budgets toward getting us to part with our money. One way this is done is to play on our sense of self-worth. To be good enough, we have to look a certain way, have a particular body size, wear specific clothes, have an extensive shoe collection, and use up a lot of our time getting waxed or tucked to attain this ideal image.

My own attention was captured when I was in my early teens. I was an avid reader of women's fashion magazines; it was the next natural step from reading girls' comics. I thought it was the epitome of being a grown-up and looked forward to the beginning of the month when I could collect my copy of *Vogue* from the newsagent at the end of the street and then spend the rest of the day leafing through the pages, gazing at the images. It was part of my education of how to be a woman, what was expected of me, how I needed to show up.

One day I was reading *Elle* magazine, when all of a sudden I noticed that there was no substance to it, just page after page of advertising, and while there was usually one in-depth article, the rest was a regurgitation of the same themes that perpetuated a sense of inadequacy and lack of worth in me. To set aside those magazines and stop wasting my time and money with them was a moment of liberation. The occasional engaging and informative articles were not worth wading through everything else that perpetuated this myth of beauty—that I had to wear this dress or that particular makeup to be valued.

Setting aside those magazines closed off a significant marketing channel for companies that wanted me to acquire their stuff and with it an onslaught of messaging that told me how to be as a woman. Now I tend to live a reasonably minimalist life, and looking after what I do have is enough for me. I don't want to be part of an economic growth worldview that requires me to consume a huge and unnecessary number of items just to prove that I'm worth loving, worth caring about. I stopped consuming in that way, and I am still loved.

Today, with social media, the marketing channels have proliferated to the point where we are marketed to by influencers whose lifestyle we're supposed to want to emulate. Young women plug into social media to learn the social cues for acceptance and success. They end up getting guidance from the influencers who unwittingly uphold a life-threatening worldview. These influencers use a company's product—for example, makeup, clothing, cleaning products—and through this help us make decisions about what we should have in order to be better, more beautiful, and brighter. These influencers also launch their own product lines, outsourcing the manufacturing to the companies.

Kylie Jenner became the youngest billionaire in 2019 through the sale of her makeup. She outsources the making of her cosmetic line to a cosmetic manufacturer. As a member of the reality TV family the Jenner-Kardasians, she uses social media to reach and sell to her millions of followers. I wonder if in the future we'll be applauding this kind of extreme wealth, which is made at the expense of life on Earth, even if the person in question is a woman, young, and the first billionaire in her age range.

In another talk, the Dalai Lama spoke of the need for us to build trust with each other. Trust in one another makes it possible for us to cooperate and collaborate in response to the collective problems we face. A component of creating trust is the ability to empathize with another's circumstances genuinely. As we know from the work of Gina Rippon in The Gendered Brain, the ability to empathize, be compassionate, and to care is not exclusive to women; however, we do tend to be socialized for this behavior and have more access to these qualities, as well as being the ones who birth children and do what we can to ensure their well-being. Honing our ability for empathy, to walk in another's shoes and genuinely gain a sense of what life is like for them, could be another clue for the new worldview and culture we need to create.

When I was in my twenties, I had the good fortune to discover and train in the Japanese healing form of shiatsu, which is based on traditional Chinese medicine. Through my teacher Marianne Fuenmayor, I learned an empathetic approach to healing. She taught us that as practitioners we were not to try to fix the person, we were to connect with them, with the imbalance they experienced in their body, and to simple be with it, observe, and be present. Through this training, I learned to listen to people, hear their pain, and gently support them in their healing journey.

I learned to work with *qi* (chi), our life force, as it moved in channels, or meridians, throughout the body, and I experienced first hand the healing benefits of consciously working with *qi*—not only on my physical body but also on my mental, emotional, and spiritual well-being. I was required to take up a meditation practice, in order to develop my ability to be present with my own energy field and with the energy in a client's body and "listen" for what was needed in the healing session. It was also during this training that I learned the importance of being conscious of what I eat and that appropriate food choices could prevent future health problems.

We are fortunate to still have these living practices, in particular those from Asia, which focus on nurturing, cultivating, and strengthening our life force, which in China is known as *qi* and in India, *prana*. This life force appears to be connected to our breath. If you practice qigong or yoga postures, you can develop your awareness of your life force as it moves in and through you and permeates everything in nature.

In ancient times, people who cultivated their life force through the practice of these movement forms perceived and documented two fundamental qualities of energy: energy that is in motion—outward, forward in direction, and focused—and another that, while moving, has a stillness to it—inward and down, expansive and soft. These two qualities of our life force are often described as "feminine" and "masculine" energies, or as they are known in China, *yin* and *yang*, respectively.

Both yin and yang exist within all of us—women and men—and can be observed in nature. They are day and night, the side of the mountain that faces the sun and is bathed in light and the side that is always in the shade. It is the seed that grows to full flower and then brings its energy inward to create new seeds. In nature, these qualities set up a dynamic polarity that makes the cycles of life possible.

The tendency has been to conflate these energetic qualities with gender; that is, men have "masculine" energy and women have "feminine" energy. While it might be the case that women tend toward demonstrating the qualities of feminine energy more than men, this could in large part be due to the dominant culture being set up to prevent us from fully embracing our masculine energy. We need to aim for a holistic approach in practice, so that we can activate either or both qualities appropriately in any given situation. It is through this balanced flow—moving outward and active, then moving inward to stillness and reflection, the actions of giving and receiving—that we settle into our sovereignty.

Being sovereign of our life means we can bring an appropriate response to whatever we encounter, whether it is something that comes through our own creativity or that of another. Our sovereign selves live from a place of agency, able to tap into an innate knowing whether now is the moment to activate our outgoing, direct, and focused energy, or is it the moment to embrace the part of our life force in which we become still, inward listening, and reflective?

The process of becoming sovereign of our lives requires a strategic approach in which we examine all aspects of our lives; identify areas where our life force is oppressed, suppressed, or depressed; and take appropriate action to free it and allow it to flow again.

When our energy is flowing, we are authentically engaged with life. We are then free of the fear of not doing something right, or in a way that others think we should do it, or how it's always been done. We then live with nothing to lose, because we are involved in the most ecstatic experience of feeling the natural flow of our energy, and moving with it as it moves with the larger energy fields of nature. When our life force is trapped, stuck, or stagnant, our behavior is out of alignment with our natural self, and we can become depressed or suffer life-threatening illness.

When you are sovereign, you are directly living your life, with nothing in between. Your experience is not mediated through someone else—your spouse or partner, your boss or colleague. When you are sovereign, you collaborate and cooperate, but you participate fully in that, rather than going along with someone else's plan. When you are tuned into your sovereignty, life will start to collaborate and co-create with you.

Have you ever had the experience of thinking something and then, in a physical form, you encounter what you were thinking about? You think about a loved one and seconds later the phone rings, and there they are, talking to you. Or you remember you wanted to contact a friend about doing something together and then they appear at your door. This is life dancing with you.

When we step into the full power of our sovereignty, we pick up the responsibility to care for and engage with the domains of our life. Becoming sovereign of your life goes hand in hand with becoming a steward and protector of all life on Earth.

# 2

*Gathering Tools*

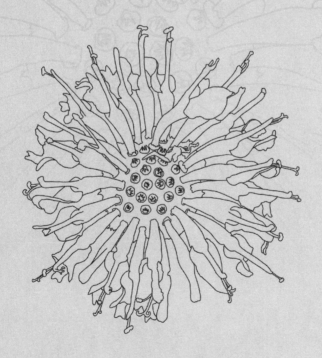

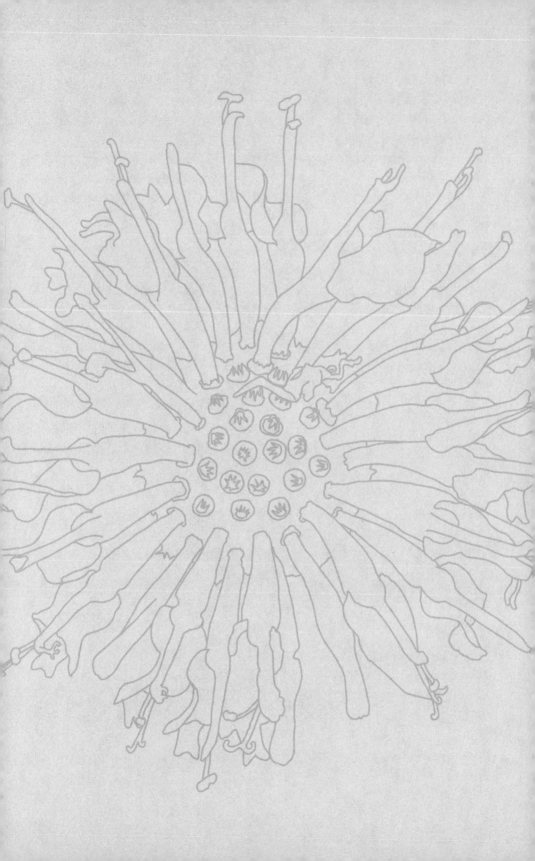

# CHAPTER 4

# Why Life Design?

Life Design offers a way for us to uncover who we really are. The process is about becoming authentic and sovereign of our lives, so that we can participate in the design and creation of wealth that goes beyond material and financial wealth and fosters genuine well-being for all beings on Earth.

We have to become a detective and an archaeologist of our own life, investigating our present through observation, and excavating our past through reflection to uncover the moments when we adopted or embodied the oppression of the economic worldview and its limited perspective of what it means to have wealth. Discovering the source of this oppression allows us to consciously choose whether to continue operating from this diminished sense of self or do the work to become free of it.

Our life is comprised of hundreds of systems, interrelated interactions that make it possible for us to live. Our physical body, for example, has 11 major physiological systems, including our respiratory, circulatory, and digestive systems. We live in homes that are set up with systems to meet our needs, such as the heating system and the kitchen—a system with elements that include a stove, sink, pots and pans, utensils, and flatware, making it possible to prepare food. We participate in larger systems beyond our homes, as we meet our needs for food and basic sustenance, livelihood, a sense of belonging and connection, understanding, and purpose. The "spheres" I mentioned earlier are nature's interconnected systems, which generate rainfall, contribute to soil fertility, and create the delicately balanced atmosphere that sustains life, and so much more.

We are continually designing systems to meet our needs. *Design* is the act of consciously arranging elements in beneficial relation to one another so that they work as a system that creates a desired output. Design can be both the process and the end result. Look around, and you will see all kinds of objects that came into existence as a result of a conscious design process— the clothes you are wearing, the furniture you sit on, the digital gadget or book you are reading these words on are all the result of design thinking. Even these words have been carefully put together using the system of language and grammar to convey ideas and create meaning. The simple act of deciding when you are going to get up in the morning and what your morning routine will be involves design thinking. This is all design.

Design is not just about creating physical objects; it can be applied to thinking about how a service is offered to a customer, how an organization is put together to function optimally, or the legal system of a country. The entrepreneur Jeff Bezos started Amazon in his garage. He didn't make a thing; he merely designed the systems by which a customer could buy a book online and have it delivered to their home. Once he had designed the system for selling and shipping a book, he was able to scale the system up rapidly to ship anything. He may not be an example of someone designing systems with the planet in mind, but he is a great example of a successful systems thinker and designer.

We need to apply our design thinking as successfully as he has, not to become multi-billionaires but to put thriving systems in place to regenerate nature for current and future generations. None of these human system designs could exist without nature's life support systems, involving a huge variety of interdependent elements working together ceaselessly, often invisible to our limited awareness to the point of us taking it all for granted.

The design of a system doesn't just happen; it's carefully considered. It starts by identifying the need or problem in the system. Information is gathered about the need or problem, and the desired outcome is defined. Then elements relevant to that system are put together in a specific way to bring about the desired result; that is, the need is met or the problem is solved.

What the global economic growth worldview does is encourage the manufacture of false problems and needs. A market for a product or service is created using powerful images of how our lives should be and then the problem is solved or the need is fulfilled by using their products or services.

A company that is modeling systemic and regenerative design in its business model is the cosmetics company Lush. The company is probably most well known for its "naked," no-animal testing, vegetarian and vegan products. For the company directors, it's not just about the end result of how good a bar of soap smells or a skin cream feels on the skin; they are fully committed to creating a supply chain that fosters natural regeneration. An example of a project they support through funding is the production of almonds for their almond oil through the regeneration of dry almond orchards. This way of growing almonds was practiced in California before the Colorado River was diverted for irrigation and the almond producers moved to water-intensive production. Sadly, with the demand on the river, it has started to dry up and no longer reaches the Pacific Ocean. Along with sourcing and supporting regeneratively produced ingredients, the company is also active in human and animal rights campaigns.

This company exists because the founders of the company had a different mindset: they wanted their business to bring well-being into every step of the production process.

We change how a system functions through an intervention. Systems thinker Donella Meadows defined what she called 12 Leverage Points, places to intervene in a system to bring about a change. The most significant and effective leverage point she identified is to intervene at the level of the mindset of people in the system.

With this in mind, Life Design is an intervention into our own mindset and way of thinking for the sake of realizing a change in the way we perceive ourselves and the world around us. We are going to actively, strategically, and systematically explore our way of thinking and unearth the roots of the mindset that keeps us defaulting to planet-destroying behavior.

After centuries of living within systems designed predominantly from the perspective of only one fraction of society—white men—it's time for people to design and implement life-giving systems that include the perspectives of multiple stakeholders and support all life on Earth.

Rather than women merely stepping into leadership roles that steer the current agenda using the same old operating system, we need to dive deeply into ourselves, crack apart the indoctrination, and discover what it is we genuinely care about, what real wealth is, and what we want to devote our lives to. I hope that the Life Design process is a supportive starting point for your journey of recovery, discovery, and lifelong learning.

# CHAPTER 5

# The Realms and Domains

The thing is, life isn't a neatly ordered, sectioned experience; it's complex and can be messy. To work with Life Design, however, we need a way to navigate the complexity. For this purpose, I organized the design process into areas of life by ordering them in relation to the level of autonomous decision-making power you have. I've called these areas "domains."

There are 21 domains altogether. They fall naturally into five groups that I call "realms": **CORE, WELL-BEING, HOMESTEAD, AFFECTION,** and **EXCHANGE.**

The following list presents the realms and domains in an optimal order for working through them, but you can work through the domains in any order that makes sense to you. You can even add domains I may not have included.

The domains are:

- **CORE:** Nature and Death
- **WELL-BEING:** Nourish, Embody, Express, Presence, Immerse, Play, Create, and Adorn
- **HOMESTEAD:** Home, Stuff, Digital, Transport, and Land
- **AFFECTION:** Family, Friends, and Intimate Companion
- **EXCHANGE:** Livelihood, Money, and Community

I chose to put **Nature** and **Death** together in the **CORE** realm to emphasize their importance and to encourage you to explore your relationship with these two domains first.

The eight domains of **WELL-BEING** that follow are those aspects of your life over which I hope you have considerable control. The first four are essential domains to work in—**Nourish:** the choices you make about the food you eat; **Embody:** your body and how you nurture it; **Express:** your emotions; and **Presence:** your process for being in the moment, in flow and connected to spirit. The next four Well-Being domains are the foundation of your Life Design—**Immerse:** the things you do to develop your thinking and your mindset; **Play:** how you unwind and let go; **Create:** that part of yourself that makes a unique expression in the world; and **Adorn:** how you express yourself through clothing and accessories.

Next come the **HOMESTEAD** domains: your **Home,** your **Stuff,** your **Digital Footprint,** your **Transport,** and your **Land.** The amount of control you have in these domains will depend on your living situation. If you live with others and want to bring about change, you will have to collaborate and perhaps find ways to inform and educate those around you in order for them to understand why you want to make these changes.

The **AFFECTION** domains focus on your relationships with people: your **Family** of origin, your **Friends,** and your **Intimate Companion.** **EXCHANGE** has three domains: the first, **Livelihood:** focuses on your work in the world; and the second, **Money:** on what you do with the money you earn. The final domain **Community** is an invitation for you to explore how you can make a more significant impact by creating change through collaboration with others.

In order to clarify the aspects of your life you will want to reflect on in the domains, I introduce each one with some broad brushstrokes. Generally, I include the reasons why a particular domain is essential for our unlearning, regenerative Life Design process. I also mention some of the challenges that exist in this domain and will only get worse for us and the planet if we continue to live the way we do. A whole book could be written for each domain; in fact, there are already plenty of books available dealing with most of them.

For the most part, it is not my intention to offer solutions or tell you what you need to do to make changes in the domain. That is for you to discover through your Life Design process, as our life situation is different for each of us. At times, I may signpost some directions you could explore. Consider the longer introductions I give for each domain in Part 3 of the book as delicious morsels in a tasting menu—just enough to whet your appetite and stimulate your thoughts and memories.

Thankfully, all aspects of your life are interconnected and influence each other. As you work in one domain, you will find that you might get ideas or make connections for another, and when you actually make changes and recover your life force in a domain, this might beneficially impact another.

Something to consider is that each domain is a field of energy that has accumulated over time. The domain is infused with everything that has ever been done, thought, or felt about it. It is your domain, and yet it also belongs to every other human being on Earth. Some people are working consciously and positively in the domain, and others are unaware of its existence. The domain is informed by the past, present, and future.

Your energy naturally circulates freely in your personal version of the domain, but if somewhere in your past you had a negative experience, your energy may have become stuck. This stuck energy will continue to manifest as life-diminishing thoughts or behaviors. Each and every moment you think that thought or do that thing, you are wasting your life force. Each and every moment you spend trying to suppress the painful feelings associated with them, you are consuming your life force. The Life Design process is intended to free up your life force so you can become a conscious life-giving contributor to that energy field.

It may be that some of the changes you make you do for yourself, with yourself. For other domains, you may be collaborating with loved ones, or you may bring in professional support from people who have experience working in that particular domain. You don't have to go it alone.

## Four Stages of Learning and Unlearning

Everything in nature is constantly changing, and as we are nature, we need to get unstuck and align ourselves with this truth. The Life Design process is about making conscious changes in your life, small ones and large ones, to move to a way of living that is in service to nature and all of life.

Making changes can be scary; change invites the unknown as well as possible risk into our lives. What if the change we make is no better than what we have now? What if I change and I feel pain, or even die?

The thing is: If we don't change, in the long run nothing will be better. Our fear of change can get us into life-diminishing ruts in which we while away our lives. The current world situation demands we get out of that rut and engage with life.

The changes you make must be conscious, strategic, and have a lasting impact. To ensure that you aren't making random guesses about what you might change, the Life Design process will help you to strategically focus on key areas of your life and create a more profound change.

In this process, you will recover your life force and become sovereign of your life. You will become nature's ally rather than its unwitting enemy. The process involves unlearning the conditioning you took on at various stages in your life. With this process, you are the one who gets to choose what and how to change. This involves unlearning old ways of doing things, so there will be room enough for you to learn new ways. The process of learning can be uncomfortable. You might feel awkward as you flail around in the unknown; in a world full of pressure to be on our game and perfect, most of us resist that space of not knowing.

Learning a new habit or skill has four stages of development. Before we even begin something new, there's a stage in which we don't know that it's something we need to know or be able to do; we are *unconsciously incompetent*. When we start the learning process, we become aware of what we don't know; at this stage we are *consciously incompetent*. This is the most uncomfortable stage of change and learning. After a time of practicing our new habit, skill or pattern, we start to be *consciously competent*. We're in our stride and feel more confident. If we persist, we will arrive at a place in which we become *unconsciously competent*. We've embodied the knowledge or skill, we've changed, and we don't have to think about what it is we're doing.

Learning to ride a bicycle is an excellent example of these stages. We begin perhaps not even knowing that bicycles exist. When we get on one for the first time, we can't even manage to balance on it, let alone move forward. Our focus is entirely on our shaky, wobbling process, and it's awkward. All of a sudden, after some practice, we're gliding along, confidently stopping and starting and taking in our surroundings. We've embodied the skill and can use it without having to think about it.

By stepping into Life Design, you may find that you go through these four stages many times. It's going to be worth it. You will reap the rewards by gaining more energy, by discovering yourself and by becoming a sovereign steward who acts in service of all life on the planet. With so many potential learning curves it's helpful to have a design system you can use to pace yourself and take on one or a few changes at a time.

# CHAPTER 6

# The Life Design Process

The Life Design process is a five-step process that guides you to examine your worldview and values in your domains. The five steps are: **OBSERVE, REFLECT, ENVISION, DEFINE,** and **ACT (OREDA)**.

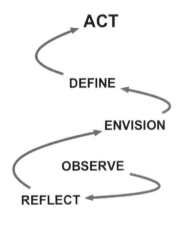

OREDA Spiral

### Observe and Reflect

When you **Observe**, you begin to explore your chosen domain, starting in the present by observing your life as it is now. In **Reflect**, you shift your focus to your past to excavate events and beliefs that might have shaped how you do things now. It may seem easier and quicker to jump into thinking about the future you, but this observation and reflection will help you become aware of your ways of being that keep you doing more of the same when it comes to the next step.

Observing our present and reflecting on our past is an essential practice of the Life Design process. It's what creates the dynamic tension between how our lives are now and the future sense of self. Observation and reflection give us the opportunity to see what's really going on in our lives, to look at where we're on track and where we're off. This practice also gives us the spaciousness to step back from the desired future outcome we think we want and go a bit deeper, asking ourselves, *Is this really it? Or is it the worldview of an old self that's fueling the desire?*

Observation and reflection create your Life Design feedback loop. You see where you are now, you make a change, live into it, and reflect: *How is this? How do I feel? What do I notice?*

Observation and reflection need time, like the growth of an oak tree, or they can happen in the flit of a bird's wing. In the Life Design process, you will initially have to dive into each domain and give yourself some time to observe where you are now, and reflect on what occurred in the past to bring you to this place.

## Envision

**Envision** is where you cast yourself into the future, and imagine the life you will live as your Sovereign Self. This process, imagining your future self, is a way to anchor your energy and intention for the direction you want to move your life in. You may have come across this practice of imagining your future in other methods.

What is different in Life Design is that the Envision step comes after you've generated insights about your present and past, and these insights are used to inform your vision of your future self. You are no longer blindly opting for an ideal future self promoted by external sources that are intended to perpetuate a narrow view of wealth, but rather seeing an authentic you rooted in the treasure you've discovered.

You will project yourself into the future and describe how you feel, what you have and are doing, and where you are living the change in that particular domain. Through this process, you are energizing your Sovereign Self and creating a vivid picture of what you want to become. If you like, you can use images to create a collage of your Sovereign Self.

## Define

Once you've completed the first three steps for a particular domain, you move on to **Define**. This is where you will define the changes you want to make to become the Sovereign Self you've envisioned and a specific change you will Act on. In this step, you will gather all the ideas you have for taking action in this domain. Then you will hone in on one activity and define what you will be doing, why you are doing it, where, when, how, and who with. You will Map for Action in order to identify the optimal time in the coming 6–12 months to begin your change process. To help you keep going, you will also identify your support networks and the ways you are going to track your change.

## Act

The next step is to **Act.** In this step, you are actually living the change. The change is made up of daily habits and practices. Tracking is a great way to see if you are actually implementing the new habit or pattern as much as you had planned to. You might be surprised to see what you think you do compared to what you actually do when you start to track your habits. Once a habit becomes embodied, you just do it without trying and don't need to track it anymore.

I no longer track coffee drinking because I've pretty much stopped. I do track the amount of water I drink because I tend not to drink enough and I know that when I do drink water, my internal body functions can do an optimal job; that is, I have fewer aches and pains, can think more clearly, and have more energy. Tracking how much I hydrate myself helps me see the correlation between my water intake and my physical well-being, and I can see whether the amount I think I drink is aligned with what I actually drink.

## Thought Seeds

At each step, thought seeds support you as you begin exploring your domain. A thought seed is an incomplete statement that you complete in your own words. There's no one right response; thought seeds are simply there to get you started. I find that they help me get into my flow more than a question. The following are examples of a question and a thought seed to show you the difference between the two:

**QUESTION:** What is your relationship with food?
**THOUGHT SEED:** My relationship with food is . . .

I chose to use a metaphor from nature—seed—for this method. Just as plants, flowers, and fruit grow from a seed, so too will your ideas, memories, and inspirations grow from the thought seeds.

For the Observe and Reflect steps, I provide both questions and thought seeds. In some domains there are just a few thought seeds, while in others there are many. Choose one or a few to work with. For the remaining steps, you will work with the thought seeds provided. During the process you may find you want to create additional thought seeds.

## Word Clouds

As you go through the design steps of Observe and Reflect in Part 3, in each domain you will notice word cloud illustrations. The purpose of these are to give you words that might help to expand the way you think about these domains. Some of the words relate to specific methods or concepts, which you can use as starting points for online research.

# CHAPTER 7

# Tools to Apply along the Way

Choosing to change, to transform, no matter how consciously you do it, is challenging; maybe it's even more challenging when you do it consciously. Gathering supportive tools or attitudes can help you stay connected to your process as you face resistance or self-doubt. The first two tools I want to bring to your attention as part of your design process are an inevitable part of your life; they are inherent. The following six are not a given, but cultivating them will help your transformation process. The final tools are the practice of journaling and the Spider Web Assessment, a quick way for you to gauge which domain you might explore first.

As a Life Designer, you need to take into account things that are inherent in the system you are designing. Something that is inherent in a system is either essential or permanent; you have to factor its existence into your design. The presence of the sun and the energy it provides, making life on Earth possible, is inherent in our planetary system. Without the energy from the sun, the wind wouldn't blow, the currents in the sea would cease, there would be no daylight, and plants couldn't grow. The planet would be cold and dark, and a different kind of life would exist here. It's easy to take for granted things that are inherent in a system. Two precious ones we all have are our breath and time.

## Breath

Our breath is inherent in our respiratory system and makes living possible. Most of us probably take it for granted. It miraculously happens without us having to think about it, and yet if it didn't happen, we would die. What we can change about it is its quality. The quality of our breath has an impact on our well-being. Simply taking a fuller, deeper breath is a substantial life-transforming step. Becoming aware of your breath, how shallow or deep you breathe, when you hold your breath, and choosing consciously to bring more oxygen into your body, is a tremendous first act.

Your breath is the cornerstone of Life Design. You can make changes in all areas of your life, but if you hold your breath or only bring oxygen into the top of your lungs, you are limiting your potential for transformation. It's often the case that beneath a tendency to take shallow breaths or to hold it are emotions we don't want to let out. Finding a safe place to take a deeper breath and let those emotions out is a regenerative practice that will help you become more grounded and connected to your environment.

Your breath is your ally on this journey. You can have as much oxygen as you wish; make good use of it. We're being sold water in bottles. What next? Our air becomes so polluted that we have to buy canisters of oxygen so we can go about our life. This is already happening in China, where the air pollution from producing products to sell to us is so bad that those who can afford it are using oxygen canisters. The leading cause of death in China is cancer caused by air pollution.

Consider bringing a regular breath practice into your life, one that gets you taking fuller, deeper breaths more often.

### Time

So often I hear people say they are busy, and I find myself saying the same thing. That got me reflecting. What am I busy with? How do I use my time? Time is inherent in our life system, inasmuch as the whole world has adopted the 24-hour clock and anywhere on this planet we have a period of daylight and a period of darkness. We all have 24 hours. Within every 24 hours, we sleep, eat, and move our bodies to stay alive. Recognizing that time offers us limits and potential helps us to think well about our Life Design.

There are seven 24-hour periods in a week. That's a total of 168 hours. Let's have a rough look at how we use that time. We might use around 50 hours for sleep, and another 25 hours for food, including shopping, preparing, eating, and cleaning up. If we are working in full-time employment, that's a 40-hour week, and then there's perhaps another eight or so hours for commuting, maybe more. What we're left with is around 45 hours a week—45 precious hours for time with family, friends, exercise, relaxation, and creativity.

Becoming aware of how we use our time, what we choose to focus on, and what we choose to do in that time is part of the Life Design process. It's not necessarily all about keeping busy. Some of the most productive use of my time is when I'm zoning out, seemingly wasting time. What I find is that those zoning-out moments are a necessary part of my creative, regenerative process. On the other hand, an activity with a defined time frame can bring about great results.

When you start to plan your Life Design actions, being conscious of how much time you have will help you to be realistic about what's possible for you to act on in a day, a week, or a month. When you understand that you have a set number of hours already spoken for, leaving about 45 hours for you to do with as you wish, you can be more thoughtful about how many changes you will take on each month or how you can design them into things you're already doing.

You may design changes that involve an hour of exercise per day, a house decluttering project, a change in your diet that involves researching and learning new recipes, and cycling to work. If you start all of these changes in the same month, you might end up feeling stressed as you have no time to relax and just be.

Understanding how much time you have and how to use it is part of the Life Design process. You can gain a clearer picture of how you use your time by tracking your activities. At some point, you develop a sense of how much time you need to do something, and you won't have to track it so much. You will just have an inner sense of what you can commit to and what you need to schedule for the future. This is essentially a regenerative, life-affirming skill to develop. Showing up on time for yourself and others shows you care. Understanding how much time you need to get something done means you minimize stress and can keep to your commitments.

## Values

The Life Design process invites an examination of our values. Pinpointing values can be hard. The way we see them is through what we do with our time and energy. If our life is precious and we only have so many hours in a day, a week or a year, then I hope we are doing what we value the most. The tricky thing about values is that sometimes you have to dig a little deeper to find what you value. You may see two people playing a team sport and if you asked them what they value, why they put energy and time into playing the game, you might hear from one that they appreciate the outdoor physical exercise as a primary value and the second person might value the team aspect, connecting and cooperating with other people.

In Life Design, what we're doing is going through all your life domains to make sure you are living what you value, rather than blindly living and acting out the values of a parent, a sibling, or society; but we're also checking to see if your values actually align with supporting a future for life on Earth.

## Curiosity

Curiosity is an essential attitude to invoke in Life Design and is an inherent part of a growth mindset. Being curious about who you are, about others, and about trying new ways of doing and being is all part of the Life Design process. If you approach your life with curiosity, you will find yourself in the heart of the design process rather than continually standing on the edge trying to get started. You will get stuck or paralyzed at times, but when you remember to tap into your curious self, you will begin to move again. I am frequently paralyzed in my transformation process. Without fail, when I start to ask questions, to wonder, to dig deeper, to find what is keeping me hooked to an old way of being or doing, something in my life force begins to flow and a shift happens.

## Compassion

When you begin this work you are going to experience challenges, times when you want to run away or dive under the covers to hide from the process. This is where you need to develop compassion for yourself. This doesn't mean you let yourself off the hook. It means that when you do run away, you give yourself space to recover and then return to the part of the Life Design process that made you want to run in the first place.

When you start to act for life, you will begin to see all the ways your life up until now worked against life. You'll see how people around you continue to act against life. The last thing we need is to become paralyzed by our shame or guilt about our behavior or get caught up in pointing fingers. The choices we made or other people are still making happen because we live within a system dominated by a worldview that funnels us into a destructive way of living. We are all compromised; yet we all believe we're doing the right thing, because it's hard to see the interconnections of everything, and it's challenging to discern the facts from the marketing hype. What could you do to develop your skill of compassion for yourself and for others?

## Fun

Somewhere along the way, I heard the phrase "If it ain't fun, it's not sustainable." Fun is an essential attitude to cultivate as you redesign your life toward one that is more conscious and life-affirming.

It's important to recognize that fun is personal. What may be fun for you may be someone else's idea of misery. As you begin to explore and take action in the direction of caring for the planet and shifting to a life-affirming way of life, you'll find that some of the solutions you arrive at involve time.

I wanted to further reduce the amount of plastic packaging coming into my life and going out into the landfill trash can, so I started to make home-made versions of store-bought foods that are packaged in plastic containers. This made sense to me because I enjoy preparing food, so I just added extra time to my fun time in the kitchen for making dips, spreads, and other items. If you don't like being in the kitchen, this is not going to be a sustainable solution for you.

What's underlying the attitude of fun is something more profound. Fun is the activity that you do willingly and with enthusiasm. While fun is about finding light-hearted activities that might initially engage you in new ways of living life, joy is the invitation to seek out that which gives you a more profound sense of pleasure. If you can find this place, you will be in a zone of self-regeneration.

What do you do in life for fun? Is it life-diminishing or life-affirming for you? For the planet? If it's life-affirming for you and diminishing for the planet, how could you adapt it so you can keep having fun doing it while including the planet's well-being in your activity?

## Edges

Edges are rich and rewarding places to explore and occupy. I remember noticing at some point in my life that the people, places, and things that were considered marginal often enriched my life. That became one of my north stars in terms of life experience. It's what took me to work in community gardens in the South Bronx and to teach English to immigrant workers from South and Central America. It's what brought me to South Dakota to learn from the Lakota people how to relate more consciously with the natural world around me. All these people and situations that are pushed off to the edge by mainstream society have a power and authenticity that comes through other ways of living and perceiving the world. These ways threaten the dominant model, so they are marginalized, to the point of elimination at times.

Later, I learned that in the ecology of natural systems, the edge is abundant in diversity and therefore the most resilient and life-giving place. One of the most vibrant edges in nature is the place where the forest meets a field. There is so much going on there. As the shaded part of the forest becomes exposed to sunlight and rain, more growth can take place, which provides more food and a habitat for insects, birds, and other animals.

In the realm of personal development there's an expression: "to be on an edge." It means that we are on the edge of our comfort zone and experiencing a sense of inner tension. This usually occurs just before a moment of inner growth, during which we integrate a part of ourselves we were unconscious of. Going consciously toward an inner edge and working with it helps us live more fully switched on, engaged, and alive in the world. Working in the area of your edges can be daunting, but if you're willing to stay with it and work through it, you will inevitably gain wisdom and more life force.

An attitude of valuing the edges you encounter, both around and within you, will support you as you work to inhabit a more life-affirming life. Things that are seen as "edgy" look threatening because they are unfamiliar, yet they carry a huge potential for transformation. Seeking out an edge and working with it could be an approach that moves you exponentially. In fact, this whole Life Design process is an invitation for you to become an edge worker.

## Begin

As part of my work, I collaborate with both individuals and groups on a range of projects, often in the role of facilitator. At times, when the group is moving toward action, I notice that people get caught up in talking about doing the action rather than simply doing it. The conversation will circle around like leaves blown into a corner by the wind, constantly being whipped up and never settling. It's as if we've agreed to go swimming together, yet we're hanging out at the edge of the lake, never daring to actually go in. It is a fascinating phenomenon to notice, and it is also how people and groups can lose energy to actually act.

Well, we need to dive in! Life wants us to get in and splash around in those delicious, cool waters with unknown depths. At some point we need to begin, because it's in the beginning that life can show up and meet you. It's in the beginning that all kinds of synchronistic events occur, like the meeting of nodes in a dynamic network.

In 2000, I was standing by the hospital bed of a friend who had been admitted as a result of a life-threatening asthma attack. We were chatting in an awkward way about a project we were collaborating on, but my younger self didn't know how to be in the presence of someone who had almost died.

All of a sudden his bed sheet became a magician's cloak from which he pulled out a small piece of paper on which were written some words by W. H. Murray about the importance of committing to action, that once we do that then "a whole stream of events issues from the decision, raising in one's favor all manner of unforeseen incidents and meetings and material assistance, which no man could have dreamt would have come his way."

I was on the brink of starting Camino de Paz, a project of making labyrinths in New York City, and clearly, this was a friendly prompt to just do it. So I did. I can attest that, as a result of taking up such an unusual occupation—an environmental and spiritual endeavor in the heart of New York City—"a whole stream of events" occurred over and over, which made bringing labyrinths to the city happen with an amazing grace and adventure. Beginning led to the creation of the Labyrinth for Contemplation in New York City's Battery Park, which continues to be sought out and walked by labyrinth lovers from all over the world.

These experiences of grace happened after a period of life reflection and questioning my worldview, then being given a clear prompt from life on what to commit to. I hope that by committing to this Life Design process, starting with bringing clarity and order into your daily life, you will begin to perceive what dance life is inviting you to join.

Beginning is about inner commitment. That's the crucial point here. In the deepest part of your being, you need to connect energetically with what you wish to engage with and commit yourself to it, then the flow will come.

## Journaling

Journaling using the thought seeds is the core practice in Life Design. The writing process invites the relationship with your inner and outer selves to develop. When you journal, you are journaling for you; this is your process of discovery.

You will find that new ideas and thoughts will come up as you write. You may even find yourself writing things that at first don't make sense. It's essential to set your inner critic and self-censor aside when you do this work. The process and your journaling are not done for anyone else, so don't worry about it making sense for anyone but you. Do make sure you can read your handwriting, as you will be referring back to what you write.

I want to encourage you to write with pen and paper rather than type. There is something about the process of writing on paper and away from the screen that evokes inspiration. As I wrote this book on the computer, I kept a handwritten journal as a way of thinking my ideas through. Frequently, it was while I was writing by hand that insights would come, which I was then able to include in the book.

Of course it might be that you have developed an inspired process through typing, and if it suits you well, then continue with it. There's nothing worse than someone enthusiastically telling you to change what's already working for you and be put off your stride as a result.

For each part of the process, there will be thought seeds to get you started. This is to be a fluid process, and as we have quite a bit of ground to cover, with 21 domains to visit, I suggest that you keep each step to about a page in your journal, unless of course, you've struck a rich inner vein and have a lot you want to bring up and out.

I use an A5 journal that has numbered pages and an index. I allocate 10 pages to each domain for the full Life Design process and keep track of where they start by putting the page number in the index. This page structure helps to keep me moving forward with the process by limiting how much I can write in each domain.

**Observe** and **Reflect** usually take about one page each, and then another page or two for **Envision**. For **Define**, I use three pages: one for gathering all the possible actions I could take to bring about change, the second for defining which change I'm going to commit my attention to, and the third for the specific action steps for **Act**. Then I have a few pages left over if I need more space.

The size of your handwriting may mean you use more or less paper. What I'm really pointing to here is to give yourself a frame—pages or time—otherwise, you could spend all your time on the domains at the beginning, and by Domain 15 you might have run out of steam. Or when you refer to your journal for the changes you want to act on, you find you've written a tome and there's too much information in it to easily retrieve the ones you committed to.

Don't worry about missing something by keeping things succinct. Life has a wonderful way of putting the things you need to pay attention to right in front of you. In this process, it might be what I call a "pop-up thought" related to a specific domain that keeps popping up as you go about your day. When that happens, you know you need to write it down and include it in your design process. This Life Design process goes deep and will take time. You can work through all the domains, or focus on the ones you know you need to evolve. If you do choose to work through all the domains before moving on to **Act**, you will gain a comprehensive picture of your life, and from there you can strategically pinpoint where to begin taking action.

The journaling alone will initiate change.

This Life Design process will provide you with a map that could keep you going for at least five years, possibly for the rest of your life. Of course, the map will change as you make changes in one part of your life, and other domains will naturally evolve. You can keep the Life Design process alive by reviewing the process once a year and seeing how your thoughts, habits, and patterns have changed.

## Self-Assessment Using the Spider Web Tool

Before you begin the Life Design process, use the intuitive tool I call a Spider Web to get a sense of where you are in each domain on a scale of 0–5. This simple scoring practice might give you some indication of where you need to put your attention.

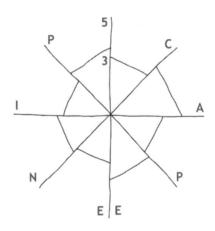

Spider Web Tool

In your journal, draw the Spider Web, and initial the triangles with the letters of each domain, as shown in the diagram. Make the same number of triangles as domains you want to score. For example, if you want to do a general overview of the seven primary domain categories, make a web with seven triangles.

For the scoring, 0 is at the center and 5 is at the outer edge. You can write the numbers along one of the spurs if you wish. I've written up a key for what each number represents. You can use it as is or adapt it to suit your needs.

| KEY | |
| --- | --- |
| 0 | This isn't an active domain in your life; you've given it no attention whatsoever. |
| 1 | You've neglected this domain or some core aspects of it; you keep going around in the same degenerative patterns, and make no progress. |
| 2 | You feel frustrated; you've tried to make changes, but nothing sticks. |
| 3 | You are beginning to make changes, but it's slow going. |
| 4 | You feel content with your energy level in this domain, but you know there's more you could do. |
| 5 | You feel fulfilled and accomplished; you are at the height of your ability in this domain. |

We'll use a highly effective internal gauge for scoring this process—your gut instinct. Simply feel into the domain as you reflect on the question: *How am I doing in this domain when it comes to contributing to a thriving future for the planet?*

Plot the number that comes up for you along one of the spurs. From that point, draw a line from one side of the triangle to the other. Continue doing this for each domain you wish to score. You could also use a compass set for drawing the lines, if you'd like. I find that easier, and I personally like the curved line. Both methods will work.

Using the Spider Web assessment tool will highlight which are the obvious domains to begin your Life Design process with. Keep your Spider Web where you can see it. You could either create it in your journal or on a separate piece of paper that you could hang on a wall so you can refer to it. Remember that this scoring is a personal assessment intended to give you a starting point, not for comparing yourself with anyone else.

How you score yourself might be different if you asked yourself a different question, which might be an illuminating exploration. The following two questions might result in a different score in the same domain.

1. How am I doing in my Nourish domain?

2. How am I doing in my Nourish domain when it comes to contributing to a thriving future for the planet?

After you've completed your scoring, choose the domain you want to work on. At the top of the page, write down one or a few points about the domain, to help you remember why you scored yourself that way. I notice that when I do the scoring process, as I'm drawing the line, at least one reason for that scoring comes to mind and then I can recall them before I start the Observe or Reflect step.

For example, as I was scoring my realms, I scored Homestead as a 2.5, which is odd because on the whole my living situation is life-affirming. When I took the next step of scoring the five domains in Homestead, I saw right away that it was the domains of Land and Digital that pulled the overall score to 2.5. I scored both of these domains at 2.5 while the others were 4 or higher. As I was drawing the line for Digital, a flurry of thoughts came as to why I was scoring myself at 2.5. The main one was too much time working at the computer. When I worked on my Digital life design, I wrote that at the top of the first page so I could remember it.

Approach the scoring process in a light manner, spending just a few minutes on each domain.

Now that you have a sense of the importance of doing conscious strategic work in your life, with some tools to support your approach, let's dive deeper into the domains and begin the Life Design process.

# 3

## *Life Design: Diving into Your Domains*

# CHAPTER 8

# Observe and Reflect

Observe and Reflect are the first two steps in your Life Design process. Using the thought seeds and other questions to prompt your journaling, you can observe how you are currently living and reflect on how you learned this way of doing things.

You can begin with Nature, which is part of the Core realm, or go to the domain you want to focus on now.

**CORE REALM**

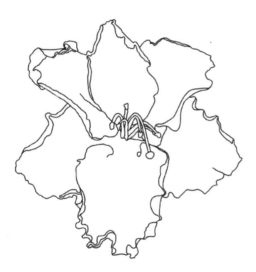

The Core realm is comprised of your Nature and Death domains. These domains come first because, in our economically driven lives, we often neglect them. It is common for Nature to be forgotten entirely and for the topic of Death to be avoided.

As part of our Life Design, we need to give these two domains proper attention and priority.

### NATURE

The Nature domain invites you to explore your relationship with nature. Nature is everything in our physical environment that is not made by us. Of course, this includes us, but for this domain we will focus on everything but you. You will focus on your personal expression of nature when you work in the Well-Being domains. We have developed a way of life that puts nature in the role of unending resource provider and backdrop. We can put nature in that role because so many of us have forgotten that we ourselves are nature and have stopped genuinely interacting with it. In the drive to make life easier and meet our needs more conveniently through mechanization, robots, and chemical enhancement, to name but a few of our technological advances, we've lost our relationship with nature. We are disconnected from it and take its existence for granted.

In the Introduction, I briefly mentioned the principles of nature that make up what we call "eco-literacy." By developing our eco-literacy, we can begin to shift our thinking of planet Earth as an insentient machine, with parts we can take out, to Earth as a living whole, of which we humans are one element of a multiplicity of interwoven and interactive relationships. We know so little about this vast and magnificent planet, and we certainly don't fully understand the intricacies and intimate relationships among the myriad living creatures that contribute to its existence. All the life-forms that participate in creating what we call nature have their own inherent purpose and reason for existence. As they live, their actions are shown to be mutually beneficial for other life-forms they relate with. In countless ways, we are among those beneficiaries. We need to find ways of reclaiming our sense of wonder and reverence for nature.

Nature is our life-support system. The four main elements of this system that make our lives possible are Air; Water; Earth, including soils and minerals; and Energy, primarily from the sun but also from nonrenewable and renewable sources, such as oil and solar, respectively. Everything we do to exist involves these elements. Without them, there is no air for you to breathe, no water for you to drink. There is no soil to grow plants for your food and clothing. There is no energy for you to heat or cool your home or to fuel your car. There's no energy for companies to extract materials from the earth for construction of the road network, housing, and the internet. Nature makes it possible for us to live on Earth. One clear example I'm so often humbled by is our reciprocal relationship with trees. They contribute to the air we breathe through the work they do, transforming carbon dioxide into oxygen.

The challenge we currently face is that many of the intricate inter-related activities nature carries out and that we benefit from are over-whelmed or collapsing due to our actions. For years, environmental visionaries have been doing all they can to communicate to the rest of us that we need to live in a way that sustains the natural environment. People who benefit financially by us not hearing and responding have blocked this message or distorted it, and now we are in this emergency situation.

Fortunately, there are people who are doing what they can to raise our awareness and put measures in place to stop further destruction of our planet. British lawyer Polly Higgins, who sadly died as I was writing this book, is one example. She switched her focus from court law to being an outspoken advocate for Earth law by seeking to have crimes of ecocide instated in the United Nations Rome Statute of the International Criminal Court, which lists international crimes against humanity. If this campaign is successful, citizens and governments will have a way to take unethical corporations, and in particular, the world's largest fossil fuel companies, to court, which would create an incentive for corporations to design the production of their commodities in a way that regenerates the planet in the process. Fortunately, through her initiative, she's left a strong cohort of lawyers and activists in place to continue this game-changing work.

The good news is that nature is still here, and we can learn from it. Nature is comprised of many systems, each one of them part of a nested circulating system that creates no waste. The discard from one element in a natural system nourishes another element. In this way energy and nutrients cycle usefully, each element playing its part in a regenerative system. This integrated way of life is what we need to implement in our lives, creating circulating systems in which, rather than throwing things out, the things we have no use for can be used by another element in our system. To take one simple example, we might contribute our daily kitchen food scraps to a compost pile as a way of participating in making nutrient rich, organic soil on which new plants can grow.

Creating an integrated life also means that we need to stop bringing items that become waste into our lives in the first place. A great deal of waste is created through plastic packaging. Plastic breaks down into microplastics that are invisible to the eye. It was once thought we could at least recycle plastic, for example by making fleece jackets from plastic bottles. Now, with the discovery of microplastics in our oceans, we see that this is not a long-term solution. Yes, we need to find solutions for the discarded plastics that are already in the system, but we need to end any further plastic production now.

We ourselves are a part of Earth, and I have a sense that, even if we are not actively engaged in acting for life, on an unconscious level we *are* affected by what's happening to the planet. Rising obesity, depression, and substance abuse are seen as health and social issues in our society, but could these problems be the symptoms of the unexpressed trauma we are experiencing as our planetary home is continually assailed at the hands of our own species?

Rewilding is an environmental movement that is gaining traction. Environmental conservation organizations around the world are working together to restore areas of natural habitat by reintroducing top predators and keystone species. We now realize that the trajectory our ancestors were on to eradicate animals that endangered their lives has systemically decimated the wilderness. The presence of a top predator brings about a remarkable regeneration of the area it's introduced in.

This was illustrated in a beautiful short film called *How Wolves Change Rivers* produced by Sustainable Human and narrated by British environmental writer and activist George Monbiot. As part of a rewilding program, wolves were reintroduced to Yellowstone National Park in 1995/1996, and the impact has been astounding and illuminating. Reintroducing the apex predator back into the system catalyzed an unfolding story of regeneration that eventually transformed the geography of the rivers. Watch the film to find out how that came about.

As part of "rewilding" ourselves, we can learn how to identify and forage the edible wild plants that grow in our area and include them in our meals. I love it when spring comes to my part of the world. The ground begins to burst with a cornucopia of wild edible greens, such as nettles, miner's lettuce, and chickweed, which I add to my salads or use to make soup or tea. I've started to encourage these wild plants to grow in my garden. Of course, if you are going to harvest from the wild, do it respectfully and sustainably, making sure there's plenty of the plant left so it can thrive.

Wild harvesting also means doing some research, not only about which plants are good to eat but also what activities have previously taken place on the land where you want to forage. Foraging on contaminated land is not going to be good for you. It's better to let the plants there get on with their clean-up work.

If you are new to the world of plants, you may want to find someone to help you learn which ones are edible. I have a friend who, when she looks at a patch of growing plants, only sees green. She finds it challenging to differentiate one plant from another at first. It can take some time to attune your eyes to see the different plants and their qualities.

Connecting with nature is a core practice for your Life Design. It can be as simple as taking off your shoes and socks to walk barefoot on the grass or diverting your run from a paved sidewalk to a park. A practice I love is to choose a place in nature that I return to again and again. Choose the same spot and spend time there observing what is happening, noticing the changes in the plants, what is growing, what has died back to make way for something else. You don't have to go far. I had a sit spot outside my back door for five years where I would sit and observe the changes. In the spring, I saw all the bright green spring tips appear on the branches of the birch tree and then watch as it gradually leafed out with a splendid cloak of green leaves in the summer. In the fall, the tree left an impression of golden streaming fireworks against the darkening sky. Low down in the winter, I saw the roe deer nibble ivy, their salad bar. In the fifth year, the strangely elongated branch planted by someone before I arrived in this spot bore apples for the first time.

Ask yourself the following questions:

- What is your relationship with nature?
- How do you connect with nature?
- What natural systems support you to live your life?
- In what ways do you regenerate your life force through your relationship with nature?
- How do you reject nature?
- What in nature scares you?

### Nature Quiz

For fun, let's find out what you already know about Nature in your local surroundings with the following thought seeds.

Consider transferring them into your journal and completing the sentences there, so you will have a record.

Give yourself 10 minutes at most to complete the sentences, and skip the ones you don't know the answer to rather than looking them up.

### Where I live

- On December 20, the sun sets . . .
  *(record the time and where on the horizon)*
- On June 20, it rises . . .
  *(record the time and where on the horizon)*
- Five native plants that grow in my neighborhood or region are . . .
- The number of days until the next full moon is . . .
- The first flower to bloom in spring is . . .
- The first flower to bloom after a heavy rain is . . .
- The nearest river is . . .
- The source of this river is . . .
- The river flows into . . .
- The soil in my region is . . .
- The total rainfall last June was . . .
- The last time there was a fire in my environment was . . .
- The direction windstorms usually come from is . . .
- The length of the growing season is . . .
- The day when shadows are the shortest is . . .
- The names of five resident and five migratory birds are . . .
- Species that have become extinct in the last 100 years are . . .

- North from where I am sitting is (point) . . .
- The water I drink comes from . . .
- After my garbage is collected, it goes . . .

Congratulate yourself for knowing what you know, and notice what you don't. You might want to take the next step and explore what you don't know. Remember, with anything in Nature, what you know is only the beginning.

## OBSERVE YOUR PRESENT

- My current relationship with nature is . . .
- Aspects of nature I enjoy are . . .
- The role of nature in my life is . . .
- Aspects of nature that I dislike are . . .
- My relationship with nature is out of balance . . .
- Ways that nature supports my life are . . .
- I bring nature into my life in affirming ways by . . .
- Life-diminishing habits I have concerning nature are . . .

## REFLECT ON YOUR PAST

- In the past, my experience of nature was . . .
- As a child, my introduction to nature was . . .
- I learned to have the relationship I have with nature now . . .
- A moment in my life I can pinpoint as shaping my current relationship with nature is . . .
- The way my current relationship with nature developed over time was . . .

## CONSIDER THE PLANET

- The impact on nature and the planet from the way I live in my Nature domain is . . .

## CELEBRATE

- Life-giving skills I have learned and developed in my Nature domain are . . .

If you are ready to continue with the **OREDA** design process for this domain, go to **Envision** on page 158.

## DEATH

The Death domain is an invitation for you to reflect on your mortality and how you lose energy through denying or suppressing the inevitability that one day you will die. What we're interested in for the Life Design process is recovering your life force by delving into any fears or other stuck emotions you may have about death. Your fears may be about your own death, or perhaps they are fears related to the loss of your mother or father, your partner, or your children. This is not about what happens to us after we die. There are different perspectives on what happens after death, and that's up to you to explore.

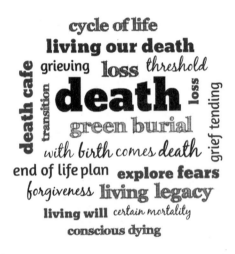

Most Western societies have developed a practice of avoiding conversations about death. In part, perhaps, this has evolved because on average we have a longer life expectancy. In the 1900s people lived into their late forties; now life expectancy is into our late seventies, almost twice as long. With a longer life, it's easy to push the fact that we will die out of our minds. When we do talk about it, people often say someone "passed away" rather than "died."

Death is inevitable, and it can occur at any time. Our unexamined fear of death unconsciously drives us to seek ways to protect ourselves from the inevitable. We strive for safety and security, usually through the accumulation of financial and material wealth, rather than exploring our fears. By exploring this domain, we can recover energy and allow our own mortality to be more present in our life. Through this, we can become more aware of what's happening around us and unfolding within us. Becoming more conscious of our inevitable death and how precious our life is might influence the choices we make.

Perhaps by becoming more present to our death, we will become more aware of the implications for other people—those close to us, as well as those who face death in challenging circumstances, such as hunger, poverty, disease, and war. Along with our feelings about dying, we might put off the practical aspects of planning for our death out of fear that attending to them will somehow bring about an early death. When someone dies, it is the grieving loved ones who have to take care of all the practical aspects. Organizing a funeral and all it entails while being overcome by grief can be a huge challenge. By giving thought in our Life Design to what we'd like done with our body and our belongings when we die, we are off to a good start in caring for our loved ones after we're gone.

When we learn more about nature, we can see that with death comes life through the cycle of regeneration. Every element that dies contributes to the life of another element. A tree falls in the forest and becomes the food and habitat for many life-forms—animals, plants, and fungi. An animal dies, and other animals feast. Microbes and other tiny soil-building creatures consume the body and turn it into nutrient-rich soil where seeds can germinate. Through observing what happens in nature, perhaps we can find ways to make peace with our inevitable death.

- In what ways have you been touched by death?
- In what ways have you explored your feelings toward your death?
- In what ways do you lose life force at just the thought of death, yours or that of a loved one?
- How have you practically prepared for your death?
- What kind of life-giving, regenerative legacy will you leave for future generations?
- What do you want to have happen to your body?
- What kind of funeral do you want?
- What do you want your body to be dressed in when you die?
- In what ways could you take a regenerative approach to your body once you die?
- What music do you want to have played at your funeral?

**OBSERVE YOUR PRESENT**

- Currently, my relationship with Death is . . .
- Death and I are . . .
- The life-affirming aspects of Death are . . .
- The life-diminishing aspects of Death are . . .
- When I lose a loved one, I feel . . .
- Recent experiences I've had with someone dying are . . .

**REFLECT ON YOUR PAST**

- As a child, my experience of Death was . . .
- Death was something my family . . .

**CONSIDER THE PLANET**

- The impact on nature and the planet from the way I live in my Death domain . . .

**CELEBRATE**

- Life-giving skills I have learned and developed in my Death domain are . . .

If you are ready to continue with the **OREDA** design process for this domain, go to **Envision** on page 158.

## WELL-BEING REALM

The eight domains in the realm of Well-Being form the foundation of your Life Design. Giving energy and time to your Well-Being self-care makes all aspects of life more enjoyable. Our Well-Being domains are the personal and intimate ones in which we should have the most decision-making power. If we decide to make life-affirming choices, both for ourselves and for the planet, we can make a significant beneficial impact, simply by living.

The first five domains are essential for life; the next two you could live without but will enhance your quality of life exponentially; the final one, you can't live without, but we tend to put too much emphasis on it.

**Nourish** is all about the food you eat and what you drink, how you nourish yourself. **Embody** is all about your relationship with your body, how you inhabit it. **Express** is an invitation to embrace your emotions, commit to learning how they inform your inner landscape, and what you can do to express them in a healthy way. **Presence** is an invitation to step into silence and become intimate with the life force that dwells within you and around you. **Immerse** is about your mindset and how you think. **Play** is about the space you give to having fun and enjoying your life. **Create** is where you bring together your imagination, inventiveness, and skills to make new things. **Adorn**, takes you back to the surface to explore the visible expression of your energized authentic self through your clothing choices.

These domains of the Well-Being realm are interconnected and work together. What you choose to eat in your Nourish domain, for example, will have an impact on your Embody and Express domains. The purpose of teasing out your Well-Being into eight domains is to give your Life Design a level of detail through which you can discover and recover more of you.

### NOURISH

Your Nourish domain is all about the food and drinks you choose to nurture yourself with. Our decisions in this domain can mean the difference between being healthy or ill, alive or dead, and our choices also have a meaningful impact on the planet.

**nutrient-rich**
*fruit* food as medicine
*vegetables* **organic**
planetary diet

# nourish

restore **compost** free-range
**food forest** *food* *locally grown*
*non-gmo* **plant-based wholefoods**
read the labels fermentation
food miles grass-fed
**biodynamic** *food waste*
**fresh water**

Food is our fuel. We have to eat to live. Food gives us the energy for all our activities—mental, physical, emotional, and spiritual. The more vibrant and vital the food we eat, the more potential we have to be vital and vibrant ourselves. Currently, however, we face a host of food-related health challenges. The health problems brought on by unconscious eating manifest in a range of forms. News reports regularly mention a rise in physical health issues like adult diabetes, heart disease, and obesity and in mental health issues such as depression, learning difficulties, and stress.

Our food choices also challenge the planet's life support systems. The way our food is currently and predominantly grown creates numerous burdens on the balancing acts nature performs to keep Earth inhabitable. Large swathes of forest are destroyed to make way for fields to grow grains to feed cattle, an industry that generates a high level of greenhouse gases, which we have now come to understand is the cause of climate change. With the trees gone, the soil is exposed and erodes. Along with erosion, the soil loses its fertility when it becomes saturated with chemical fertilizers, pesticides, and herbicides, or with chemical run-off from other industrial processes. Additionally, we are witnessing species collapse, as animals and plants lose their habitats due to our rapacious activities.

When we eat, we are literally eating the planet. We are imbibing it through our relationship with food. Consciously considering what we eat and transforming our relationship with food—the choices we make about where it comes from and how much we consume or waste—could have a massive impact. A personal change to a more healthful way of eating could have substantial beneficial and regenerative effects on what's happening to the planet.

We can choose from an abundance of food and drink, which ranges from toxic and lacking in nutrients to life-giving and nutrient-rich. It's the latter end of the spectrum we want to move toward. Our challenge is to unlearn our habits of reaching for familiar processed convenience foods and choose more fresh, unprocessed ones. My supermarket trip takes me about 15 minutes now, and for most of that time I'm in the fresh vegetable and fruit section. I've given up traveling through the other aisles stacked with processed products full of empty calories. If I do browse, I take a few seconds to read what's in the product by glancing at the label. The first item on the list indicates the highest quantity of ingredients, and so on. You might be surprised to find that a product labeled as coconut milk has more grape juice concentrate in it than actual coconut.

The life-affirming direction we need to head toward if we want our way of life to support the way of life of the planet is a predominantly plant-based diet, becoming known as the Planetary Diet. Eating this way doesn't mean you have to become a vegan; in fact, in some farming practices, animals are a necessary part of the system. When I attended a community meeting on how to respond to climate change, a woman proposed that we all adopt a vegan-based lifestyle. After she spoke, a local small-scale farmer told those present that he needed animals as part of his farming system as their manure provided essential nutrients to make the soil fertile. He treated his animals well, and after they were slaughtered, he sold them to local butchers.

We need to question our belief that eating meat at every meal is good for our health. It's only been in the last couple of generations that it's been possible to eat such a quantity of meat.

When I switched to a primarily whole food, plant-based way of eating in my twenties, my mother asked me, "Where will you get your protein from?" Growing up in 1940s post-war Scotland, she had learned that she had to feed her family meat to ensure we were all getting enough protein. I remember enjoying her homemade hamburgers, spaghetti Bolognese, and meatloaf when I was growing up.

When I left home, and after educating myself more about food, I decided to stop eating cows, sheep, and pigs. A few years later, I stopped eating chickens and turkeys. On a primarily whole food, plant-based Planetary Diet for many years, I've led a healthy and active life without meat-sourced protein. After a five-year break, I now eat fish occasionally and when possible catch it myself.

Why is meat produced on an industrial scale so damaging to the planet? Meat production and distribution systems create and contribute to climate change through the greenhouses gases they emit into Earth's atmosphere. The two primary sources are the methane released when cattle belch, and the nitrous oxide released through the use of natural and synthetic fertilizers.

Climate change isn't the only environmental damage industrial-scale farming causes. Large-scale deforestation takes place to make pastures for grass-fed livestock, and with deforestation comes erosion of the topsoil. Soils are further damaged through the overuse of chemicals, turning what was once a living soil into a dead zone. Our water is contaminated by animal waste and the runoff of agricultural chemicals washed off the fields by rainfall.

I recently met with the chief chemist for a global agrochemical company. He had realized his company needed to transition their business to support a more regenerative form of agriculture. To this end, he was looking for alternative approaches and products they could manufacture. Understandably, he was concerned with keeping the 3,500 staff members in the Europe branch employed. As we talked, he acknowledged that the current industrial-scale food production system involving the use of tons of chemicals derived from nonrenewable sources was not sustainable.

It is heartening to meet people in the industrial food production sector who are thinking this way. It will be the changes made by both the food companies and us that will make the most significant difference. We need our food production sector to move to local, regenerative agriculture, which includes practices that encourage Earth's life-support systems to regenerate while producing our food. We are in a global food crisis. It's hard to see it because we can still go to the supermarket and find boxes and packages of food on the shelves. By 2050, there will be a world population of 9.2 billion people to feed. We can't keep clearing land to produce more meat.

Food production systems must change to meet future demand while simultaneously ensuring the regeneration of Earth's life-supporting systems. Through our personal choices, we can have a significant impact on making this change happen. Cutting our meat consumption to one or two portions a week is one way we can make a difference. If everyone who eats meat almost daily did that collectively, we'd make a massive positive impact on our health and the planet's health. Moving from a predominantly meat-based diet to a whole food, plant-based one is a high-impact, beneficial choice. A whole food, plant-based diet gives your body the range of nutrients it needs while reducing the causes of climate change and other environmental degradation.

Even when we choose a predominantly whole food, plant-based diet, we need to be aware of the spectrum of our food sources, from beneficial to detrimental. Conventional farmers grow their plants with synthetic fertilizers, pesticides, and herbicides that create short-lived soil fertility and kill the microbes and other forms of life that create true soil fertility as part of the soil-food web. Local, organically grown food is the most beneficial option for your health as well as for the planet. By buying locally grown food, you reduce the amount of carbon emissions contributing to climate change, as the distance your food travels to get to you is much shorter. You will ingest fewer chemicals, and by buying organic, or at least pesticide-free, there will be less incentive for the chemical food production system.

As important as what we eat is how we eat: how we prepare food and *how* we eat it. There's a growing awareness that taking time to savor our food, to actually sit down and put our gadgets aside and be present with what we're eating, is health-giving. Make time to prepare and eat food together with family or friends. Or be silent and present with your food, so you can really taste it. Food made with love and enthusiasm sings off your plate. Preparing food at home is so easy these days as the internet is brimming with generous people sharing their recipes for plant-based meals.

Another critical aspect of how we nourish ourselves—one that will have a massive impact on relieving the pressures on the planet—is reducing the amount of food we waste. According to Dana Gunders of the Natural Resources Defense Council (NRDC) in her 2012 report, the amount of food waste in the United States is the equivalent of "walking out of a grocery store with four bags of groceries, dropping one in the parking lot, and not bothering to pick it up. That's essentially what we're doing in our homes today." You wouldn't do that, would you, abandon one of your bags of just purchased food? That is what we do once we take it home. The food sits unused in the fridge or cupboard until it has to be thrown out. Equally a problem is that use-by dates can result in us throwing out food that can still be eaten. Becoming savvy about sell-by and use-by dates and knowing how to distinguish between food that is still edible and food that has really gone off can help us cut down on the amount of unused food we throw out.

### We've explored food a little. What about drink?

The best drink for your body and the planet is water. Most of us don't drink enough water. When I feel like a wilted flower during the day, if I remember to have a glass of water, about 15 minutes later I feel restored. I loved drinking coffee and tea, but I started to notice that I felt particularly agitated and anxious after drinking a delicious cappuccino from the Italian café on the corner of the street, so I cut out the cappuccino and with it my anxiety. By the same token, when I found that I was waking up in the middle of the night, switching from black tea to herbal tea restored my restful nights. Turns out I love feeling calm and getting a good night's sleep more than the coffee or tea.

### Restore

While nourishing yourself with good food is essential for your health and vitality, so too is giving your body a break from food from time to time with a restorative process. Reducing the amount of food you eat even for a single day gives your body the opportunity to regenerate. There are various perspectives on the appropriate approach to fasting, and it's essential that you know what you're doing. You don't have to stop eating for a week. Merely reducing the amount of food you consume for a few days could make a difference to your health. For many years, my baseline way of eating has been plant-based whole foods.

A few years ago, I started a practice of juice feasting once a week. I knew how good juicing was for my health, having done juice feasts for several days at a time in the past, but my circumstances were such that juicing for any length of time wasn't possible. Since implementing the practice of consuming just green juice for a day, once a week, my health has improved, and the sore throats and colds I used to get in winter never get a hold of me, while people around me are coughing and spluttering.

I started this weekly practice after years of studying fasting and doing guided cleanses with teachers. I don't go from eating a heavy meal one day to juicing the next and back to heavy meals. On the days on either side of the juicing day, I eat vegetables mixed as a delicious salad or lightly cooked.

Along with the juicing, I go to a local sauna for a couple of hours. This is especially great for sweating out the toxins. I find that on my day of juice feasting and the day after, I have more energy and greater mental clarity.

Another aspect of Restore is nourishing your body with medicinal herbs. I love to work with herbs, drinking them as teas or taking them in tinctures or decoctions to support specific organs to function optimally. Restore is about finding the appropriate herb or herbs that will support your regenerative process.

Be loving with your body when you're restoring it. Find what works for you when giving your body a break from the constant process of digesting food. I'm relaxed and flexible about my weekly juicing. If there's a social occasion or I'm traveling, I skip the juicing or change it to another day. This flexible approach is what makes it possible for me to keep doing this beneficial practice.

In sharing my restorative juicing experience, my intention is to inspire you to get to know your body and learn in what ways you can support your body's well-being. Consult a holistic health practitioner who has experience with restorative practices, if this is a new area of health for you. Restore is not about losing weight; it's a regular practice for maintaining your health and well-being.

Feeding and hydrating ourselves in a way that both optimizes our health and is beneficial for Earth's life-supporting systems is a nuanced and complex issue. There's so much more to say on the subject. I've put Nourish first in the Well-Being domains because if we make changes here, we'll take a big step toward ensuring a thriving future. Through your reflections on your own beliefs and accompanying research, you will discover your sovereign approach to your Nourish domain.

- How do you nourish yourself with food and drink?
- Are you aware of how certain foods make you feel after eating them?
- Where does the food you buy come from?
- How is your food grown?
- How do you feel after a meal you've cooked yourself?
- How do you feel after you've eaten a TV dinner?
- Do you have any awareness of the cycles of nature through the way you nourish yourself?

**OBSERVE YOUR PRESENT**

- My relationship with food is . . .
- The way I Nourish myself with food is by eating . . .
- My life-affirming patterns with food are . . .
- My life-diminishing patterns with food are . . .
- The physical symptoms I experience in my body that could be related to life-diminishing patterns with food are . . .
- Life-affirming types of drink I enjoy are . . .
- Life-diminishing drinks I find myself turning to are . . .

**REFLECT ON YOUR PAST**

- In the past, the way I engaged with food was . . .
- In the past, the way I engaged with drink was . . .
- As a child, I learned to Nourish myself in life-affirming ways by . . .
- As a child, I learned to Nourish myself in life-diminishing ways by . . .
- Messages I received from marketing about what to eat and drink were . . .

**CONSIDER THE PLANET**

- The impact on nature and the planet from the way I live in my Nourish domain is . . .

**CELEBRATE**

- The life-affirming skills I have in my Nourish domain are . . .

If you are ready to continue with the **OREDA** design process for this domain, go to **Envision** on page 158.

## EMBODY

The Embody domain is about becoming conscious of how we enjoy and experience life in and through our physical body. Embody goes hand in hand with Nourish, each domain influencing and enhancing the other.

Our life unfolds through our bodies, when we're walking, stretching, dancing, bending, reaching, breathing, making love, relaxing, and so much more. Our bodies are home to our brain, our heart, and all our other organs and systems that make it possible for us to function.

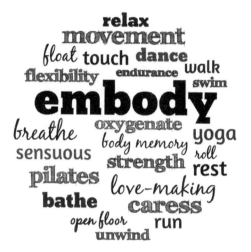

We taste the world through the taste buds on our tongue. We hear the sounds of life as they vibrate on the delicate membrane of our eardrum. Our ability to smell the scent of the world begins with the olfactory receptors in our nasal cavity. We touch, and the world touches us through the receptors of our skin. We see the visual beauty and horrors of our world through our eyes.

Further senses in our body help us to detect temperature, motion, vibration, pain, balance, hunger, and thirst. Our bodies are astoundingly miraculous designs. They transform everything we ingest into the energy that fuels their operation and maintenance. All we have to do is eat, drink, and breathe.

Our intuition, often referred to as our sixth sense, is felt in our body. You may have a "gut feeling" or perhaps feel restriction in your chest or expansion in your throat concerning a situation you're involved in. These bodily senses ensured our ancestors' survival. We feel our emotions in our body—the weight of sadness, the frisson of fear, or the flare of anger. As women, the arrival of our menstrual cycle in our early teens brings us even closer to our bodies. We become aware of changes in our bodies as our hormones orchestrate our fertility cycle. We search for solutions to alleviate physical challenges such as cramps and fatigue. Some of us may also become aware that our monthly cycle is connected to the larger lunar cycle when we bleed, as the moon becomes full or new, and that this is, in turn, connected to the tides of the oceans.

Our bodies hold memories. I've noticed that when I have a particular routine, such as keeping something stored in a specific place, say, a saucepan I often use for cooking dinner, my body takes me to the drawer where I keep it without me having to think about where it is. Or when I ride my bicycle, I don't need to think about it; I just get on and go. My body memory knows what to do. When my father's mental capacity diminished with Alzheimer's disease, his body memory helped him move through the routine of getting dressed in the morning. He wouldn't know where to begin, but if I started him off with the first step, holding the bottom of his vest in both hands, his body knew what to do next, and he pulled it over his head without any prompting from me. He then reached for his shirt and did the rest by himself.

We have made such significant gains in technology, mechanizing so many of the tasks that our ancestors had to do with their bodies. Our basic needs are met either through the gadgets and appliances in our homes and workplaces or because other people operate machines in factories around the world to make the things we need and want to make our lives easier. These helpful machines have contributed to our disembodied lives. There is no longer any fundamental need to move our bodies. Depending on our work, it is entirely possible to spend the whole day seated, moving only our fingers on a keyboard as the synapses in our brain fire. When we're finished with work, we zone out in front of another screen, watching our latest favorite series.

Embody is about designing our lives to ensure that we have an embodied experience, bringing movement in as a core well-being practice. We can invigorate our lives when we move enough to get our hearts beating and our blood pumping. You may have managed to get by with a minimalist relationship with your body until now. As we mature, the phrase "use it or lose it" becomes a truth. We need to move our bodies to maintain good health, as movement supports all our body's systems to function well.

When we increase our stamina, strength, and flexibility, interacting with the world becomes a pleasure. Physical experiences that were once challenging become easy. I give some of my time to a local nature conservation organization, and we often plant trees. My upper body strength was weak when I started volunteering, and I found the tree planting to be arduous. For other reasons, I began a regular practice of swimming twice a week. The next time our work party planted trees, I noticed how much more enjoyable it was. When I reflected on why, I realized that the swimming had strengthened my upper body, which made the work easier.

There are so many ways to get our bodies moving. Even if your time is limited, it's still possible to fit activity into your day. If you don't have a lot of time to get physical, consider joining one of the many online communities offering a wealth of activities, from aerobics and yoga to Zumba, that support you to move at home.

Another challenge that many women face is the constant search for the perfect body. This is perpetuated by the dominant worldview, which sells us an ideal beauty we are meant to measure up to, inundates us with these images, then sells us the products that will supposedly get us there—plucked, tweezed, shaved, tucked, primped, curled, and painted. The implicit message is that the skin we are born in is inadequate, and the marketing industry employs the powerful, attractive force of idealized women's bodies as a way of stimulating the desire to consume in both men and women.

Collectively, women lose millions of hours of their lives seeking relief from an artificially generated feeling of being worthless and inadequate. Millions of our collectively earned dollars, euros, or pounds are wasted paying for products and treatments intended to improve the way we look. For many, this unattainable beauty gives rise to depression and other mental health issues and self-harm in the form of bulimia. The economic growth worldview drives all of this.

If we pursue this false beauty myth, we participate in a system of production that isn't that beautiful. We buy the products, and half used or unused they pile up in our bathroom cabinets or are tossed out to join billions of other discarded products. When we throw out the products and their packaging, they either go into the landfill for future generations to uncover or they are incinerated, pouring toxic particles into our atmosphere and contaminating the air we need to breathe. For a fleeting and false beauty created through manipulated photographs, we are participating in a long-term degeneration of the air that we and future generations need to breathe. For those of us who live in areas where our garbage is buried in landfills, we contribute to the contamination of groundwater and the soil.

By developing our command over the decisions we make in our Embody domain, we gain the power to bring about much-needed beneficial changes. Let's learn to love ourselves for who we are without having to tweeze, dye, and paint. Let's allow ourselves to sink into a deep appreciation of the miracle of our bodies and all the experiences they make it possible for us to have.

I've described two aspects of our Embody domain that tend to be out of balance in women's lives: lack of movement through a sedentary life and the search for an unreal beauty. Perhaps you relate to those experiences; perhaps you don't. There are other aspects of our physical being you can consider in this domain.

### Sleep

The day after a sleepless night can be torture, especially if you have activities that need your clear and focused attention. If you want to be effective in your life, getting your sleep pattern right is essential. It's a necessary part of being able to function optimally and maintaining your health. While you sleep, your body is busy with restorative processes.

Research shows that the optimal amount of sleep is between six and eight hours a night. That's about a quarter to a third of our lives. According to the body clock model found in Traditional Chinese Medicine, it's not just about the *amount* of sleep; it's also *when* you sleep. At different times during the night, your body is performing restorative processes, from repairing and protecting your brain to cleaning your blood. Going to sleep by around 10 pm allows your organs to do their job well.

Sleep researchers have identified a 90–120-minute cyclical pattern of sleep in which your body goes through different stages. There is a stage during these cycles in which our eyes move rapidly. This phase is known as the Rapid Eye Movement phase, or REM, and it's the time when we dream.

If you wake up during or right after a REM stage, you are likely to remember your dreams. Some people find they gain insights into their waking life from their dreams.

If you're not sleeping well, either because you can't fall asleep or because you wake up fitfully during the night, it's worth exploring what could be the cause. A few years ago, I started to wake up consistently around 3 a.m., and it would take me an hour to fall asleep again. I would have to drag myself through the following day or take a nap. I hated that dragging feeling, so I took my detective lens and looked for the source of my sleeplessness. I cut out or cut down on everything that could possibly be stimulating and traced my wakefulness to the tea, coffee, or chocolate I enjoyed in the afternoon. So now I enjoy tea with my breakfast and try not to have anything stimulating after 11 a.m. If I do consume stimulating food or drink later in the day, I make sure I really enjoy it while being conscious of the consequences of my cavalier attitude toward my potentially sleepless night.

Menopause can be a big sleep disruptor. I've heard from quite a few women that they wake up at 4 a.m. and are unable to fall asleep again. They've tried everything they can think of to ensure a good night's sleep, and they still wake up at 4 a.m.

I am curious about this consistent time: 4 a.m. When I attended a meditation retreat, we gathered at 4 a.m. for the first meditation of the day. Rather than fight the wakefulness, if you don't have appointments or activities you need to be fully awake for that day, perhaps getting up and meditating is what your life force needs. You might find that meditation is as restorative as sleeping.

It could also be that your body just wants to do something different from the prescribed norm. Until the 1900s, it was common for people to sleep at least twice in a 24-hour cycle. In countries like Spain, where it's hot during the middle of the day, people have a siesta in the early afternoon and then are awake until later at night. In countries where electric light doesn't dominate, people may go to sleep soon after sunset and then wake up several times during the night. Of course, this is only possible if you don't have to be at work by 9 a.m. that day.

If we spend a third of our lives sleeping, it's also worth thinking about the setting we sleep in—the room, the bed, and the pillows and covers. Natural fabrics are usually best, as they let your body breathe.

Your bedroom doesn't need to be huge, but it is good to have it well ventilated. Also, consider the number of electric gadgets you are surrounded by when you get into bed. Other things that might cause ongoing sleepless nights are your WiFi router and any smartphones that are left on.

Even when you're not using these gadgets, they are continually sending and receiving signals that can be stimulating for some people, causing a bad night's sleep.

Sleep is essential for a good waking experience, so it's worth finding out what works for you:

- What habits do you have that prevent you from sleeping well?
- Have you noticed changes in your sleeping patterns over your lifetime?
- If you have reached menopause, do you notice a connection between changes in your hormones and your sleep?
- If you have sleeping difficulties, in what ways have you experimented with making changes?
- In what ways could you improve your sleeping environment?

- Do you have a life-affirming relationship with your body?
- What life-diminishing beliefs about your body do you perpetuate?
- Which part of your body do you dislike and need to learn to love?
- What prevents you from staying motivated to move your body?
- What about just being in your body, luxuriating in the pure joy of being a physical being?
- How does your relationship with your body reflect your relationship with the planet?
- Your teeth and eyes—how well do you care for them?
- What can you do for your posture and your joints?
- Do you know where your liver is and what it does? How can you care for it?
- What about exploring your body clock by noticing how you feel when you wake up or eat at different times?
- If you feel physically out of balance in your Embody domain, do you reach for the medicine cabinet or reflect and take life-affirming action in your Nourish and Embody domains?

Now is the time to begin designing your Embody domain. Explore through the power of observation and reflection what it is you need to do and how you need to be to reclaim or redirect your life force in ways that support you in claiming your power and designing this domain of your Sovereign Self.

**OBSERVE YOUR PRESENT**

- My relationship with my body is . . .
- The challenges I experience with being physical are . . .
- Life-affirming thoughts I have about my body are . . .
- Life-diminishing thoughts I have about my body are . . .
- Life-affirming things I do to and with my body are . . .
- Life-diminishing things I do to and with my body are . . .
- I'd like to change how I exercise by . . .

**REFLECT ON YOUR PAST**

- In the past, I engaged with physical activities by . . .
- I was inspired to Embody myself in life-affirming ways by . . .
- I was inspired to Embody myself in life-diminishing ways by . . .
- As a child, I learned that my body was . . .
- As a child, exercise was . . .
- As a child, embodied experiences were . . .
- I adopted life-diminishing thoughts about my body by . . .

**CONSIDER THE PLANET**

- The impact on nature and the planet from the way I live in my Embody domain is . . .

**CELEBRATE**

- Skills I have learned and developed in my Embody domain are . . .

If you are ready to continue with the **OREDA** design process for this domain, go to **Envision** on page 158.

## EXPRESS

Making time to design your Express domain is essential if you want a better quality of life, especially if you haven't done any work in this area until now. Emotions are part of life. We experience emotions that make us feel good and emotions that make us feel bad. We can treat them in one of three ways: suppress them, express them, or transform them. While a small percentage of people express them, what most of us do is suppress them, and when we suppress the ones that make us feel bad, we also suppress the ones that make us feel good.

emotion tracking

feeling **empathy**

emotional intelligence

# express

trigger     trauma healing

suppress **express transform**

co-counseling *emotional timeline*

conscious expression

**non-attachment**

*atlas of emotions*

Expressing our emotions is a step toward being able to transform the ones that make us feel bad, that make us feel pain, because it's the first step in acknowledging that the pain exists. The next and most life-giving regenerative step is to transform them. We will go deeper into this in the next domain, Presence. Through the Life Design process and a commitment to take action in the Express domain, our consciousness will develop and we will gain a command of the energy currently trapped in life-diminishing emotions.

It is crucial that we develop the ability to express the emotions we have defined as negative in a constructive way. Otherwise we will perpetuate life-diminishing situations by further suppression or overreacting. Other people, events, or even moving our bodies in unfamiliar ways can trigger our emotions.

When relating with people, our emotions can be triggered when they say or do something that stimulates a painful memory. The pain we experience when negative emotions are triggered is so uncomfortable that there's a tendency to react by blaming that person for making us feel bad. Our emotions can also be triggered when someone else has a strong emotion and our body memory resonates with it. When this happens, we might not want to feel that pain, so we simply ignore that this person is feeling pain and gloss over it by changing the subject or telling them to get a grip.

Experiencing pain was the way our ancestors survived. It was through experiencing physical pain that they knew to avoid putting their hand in the fire or to invent ways to clothe themselves or build shelter. Pain creates the boundaries within which we live, but these boundaries can be life-limiting, especially when the pain is related to suppressed emotions from childhood. If we avoid pain through suppressing our emotions, we are stopping the potential for joy. Or we will try to get rid of the pain by pushing it back onto others and undermining our relationship with them.

What we need to realize is that experiencing a difficult emotion is a gift, although it might not feel like it at the time. The emotion is pointing to the well of pain we've stored in our bodies during our lifetime. Through a triggering event, the emotion brings the pain to the surface, where you can work with it. It is by working with it that you can recover more of your energy. When someone says something that triggers an emotion and the connected pain, the life-giving response is to take some space and recognize that the pain we are experiencing is not something anyone has caused in this present moment. It may be difficult to take responsibility for the emotion, as the feelings of discomfort can be strong, and we have a desire to push it back onto the person who unwittingly or in some cases purposely triggered us.

Rather than looking for someone to blame, we need to find embodied ways to express our emotions. We might do this through dance or by having a pillow fight—with our pillows or a trusted friend. Choosing a physical expression will help move the energy through your body. The more thoroughly you get into it, the better. As you develop your emotion tracking skills, you might notice that at different times in your life you are working with different emotions. Once you've worked with sadness, another emotion may start to make its presence known.

An interaction with another person isn't the only way an emotion can be triggered. We can trigger an emotional experience in ourselves. The starting point of an emotion is our thoughts. If we keep thinking over and over about an event, our energy builds up, and we experience emotional sensations in our body or mind that we relate to that event. If our thoughts about the event are life-diminishing, we're more likely to feel painful emotions.

Suppressed emotions can arise when you move your body in new and unfamiliar ways, perhaps through vigorous dancing or exercise. I touched a deep well of suppressed sadness while engaged in a particularly powerful yoga practice. After each posture, the teacher would invite us to lie in Corpse pose, and after some of the positions, I found I was lying on my mat with a heavy sensation in my heart and tears flowing from my eyes and gathering in puddles in my ears. As emotionally painful as it was, I lay there and let the waves of sadness move through me. The heavy feeling went on for a few weeks and then it stopped.

We are so used to suppressing our emotions that the thought of expressing them can be scary. A huge therapeutic industry has formed to give us safe, supportive places in which to express our emotions. We need to be aware that with some therapies, we could get stuck in the "story" of what happened to give rise to the emotions, rather than focus on expressing the emotions. We tend to wrap the emotions in reasons why we have them. What we need to do instead is express the emotions whole-heartedly, as much as is needed, and let them go. If we attach a "story" to the emotions, we are merely creating another way to keep them around.

When we suppress our emotions, it can lead to misunderstanding and ambiguity when we communicate with others. We are sitting on energy that is charged with emotion, unable to express our needs. We are inauthentic in our communication, and people can sense this. They may not be skilled enough to say what's happening, but they pick up that something is incongruent.

Emotions are energy. Our life force is given a particular form through our thoughts. If we want to access more of our life force, we need to express and transform our emotions. Working with our emotions is a process that can last a lifetime.

In response to what's happening to the planet, we can be somewhere in the spectrum from completely numb to extremely emotional. Suppressing our emotions and becoming numb means that we stay in denial of the devastation taking place. We are numbed out to the fact that we are collectively participating in ecocide, which is destroying our own home and that of many other species. Extreme emotional reactions to the situation can lead to the inability to effectively respond, as the emotion overcomes us. We need to do the work of connecting with the trauma arising from the fact that we are committing ecocide and find ways to express those feelings. Through doing this work, we can become active agents working on behalf of all life on Earth.

The situation on Earth requires that we collaborate. If we are walking around full of emotional charge, it can make it challenging to work well with others. When we are triggered we can take things personally and blame other people—the ones who inadvertently triggered us. What we need to do is acknowledge the gift they have given, which is not always easy, and take responsibility for our emotions. Once we have processed the emotion, of course it could then be that we need to address the behavior of the person who triggered the emotion.

We need to develop our practice of emotional awareness by becoming emotion trackers. As emotion trackers, we create a practice of noticing when our emotions show up and what the trigger is; just as de-cluttering your home gives you physical space and peace of mind, de-cluttering your emotional field will liberate your life force. You don't need to know what the inciting incident was. As we develop our emotional awareness, we become more attuned to the emotions of others and develop the skill and practice of acknowledging their emotions and, where possible, give space for them to be expressed.

There are many different approaches to expressing and releasing emotion. We could work with a therapist specially trained to hold the space for us, who can prompt us to explore areas of our lives that might be particularly painful. We could also work with a peer in the process known as co-counseling, through which we create a safe space for each other to express our emotions in turn.

I like to look for opportunities in life through which I may experience an emotional edge, fear in particular, and set up a safe experience to face that fear. Singing is something I love to do, but when I was a child, an older friend teased me, saying I couldn't sing. Being older than me, and someone I looked up to, I took what he said as the truth, rather than just a mean dig. I was crushed by his comment and felt ashamed and exposed and developed a fear of singing in front of people.

The first step I designed to move through my fear was to sing karaoke. When I told friends what I was doing, they came along, and together we supported each other to work through our fears. As a bonus, we became part of a karaoke community, and I felt the support of the regulars when I got up for my turn. In the end, this action was particularly powerful in terms of helping me let go of my fear due to the unexpected supportive response from the people in the audience. Their encouragement and receptivity were deeply healing for me.

Most of us are experts at suppressing our emotions. We need to find life-affirming ways to express both the good ones and the bad ones, and ultimately, we need to transform them. By giving them attention, we will gain energy that we can direct toward meaningful action, whether it is personal or collective. This domain is edgy. You have to be willing to be vulnerable, open up to yourself, and step over what might feel like the edge of a cliff. Developing the skill of attending to our emotions and the pain that resides within them is a big part of becoming congruent and authentic.

- In what ways do you avoid feeling your emotions?
- What events trigger your emotions?
- Who do you blame when your emotions surface?
- How could expressing your emotions be a gift for you?

**OBSERVE YOUR PRESENT**

- My relationship with my emotions is . . .
- My emotional strengths are . . .
- My emotional weaknesses are . . .
- My current mood affects my thoughts and decision-making by . . .
- The assumptions I have about emotions are . . .

**REFLECT ON YOUR PAST**

- As a child, I learned that my emotions were . . .
- I adopted life-diminishing thoughts about my emotions by . . .
- I adopted life-affirming thoughts about my emotions by . . .
- The adults in my life considered emotions to be . . .

**CONSIDER THE PLANET**

- The impact on nature and the planet from the way I live in my Express domain is . . .

**CELEBRATE**

- Life-giving skills I have learned and developed in my Express domain are . . .

If you are ready to continue with the **OREDA** design process for this domain, go to **Envision** on page 158.

## PRESENCE

The Presence domain is all about developing a personal practice that takes you to a place of inner listening, in which you are deeply connected to your intuition, whence your authenticity and sovereignty arise. I've also included the transforming of your emotions and pain in this domain because, as you develop your ability to be in the moment, you will have the skills to be present with your pain.

contemplation
walking meditation
transform emotions solitude
stillness **connected** qigong

# presence

congruent integrity sovereign
in the moment
being power mindfulness
meditate heart-centered
reflection nature fleeting
labyrinth

Some people call that inner knowing the "still small voice within," some the "higher self," some "that which cannot be named." If you need to call it something, name it in a way that helps you to connect. The most important thing is that you are connecting. For our purposes here, the point of this connection is to help you hone your practice of authentic, right action.

With so much degeneration occurring on the planet, it is easy to get stirred into a frantic reaction in an attempt to do something about it. My invitation, as we become increasingly aware of just how messed up things are on the planet, is to embrace nonaction, pause, and become present with what is. I'm not saying don't do anything; what I'm proposing is that you carve out the time for your practice of inner listening and be still until you sense the prompting of right action rather than reaction.

When you commit to an ongoing practice in your Presence domain, you develop the ability to just be with what is unfolding in your inner and outer life. Being with events as they take place, you will use your life force most efficiently. By being with whatever arises, we might gain insights or direction for the situation at hand.

Developing Presence is also the next step in the process of working with the pain brought up by your emotions, as described in Express. In the Presence domain, you transform your emotions by being with them, merely observing them until they dissipate.

The opposite of Presence is scattered activity. The more you avoid or ignore the emotional pain that arises in your life, the greater the pain and the difficulty in resolving it the next time. Emotions, or situations that give rise to them, that are put off will inevitably return in a different form and will, most likely, be more unpleasant and painful to attend to.

Initially, Presence can be a challenging domain to develop. The idea of being, rather than doing, is counter to how we were trained since childhood. We were told that activity is what is rewarded; doing, making, producing—these were the ways of life that had value. Through this conditioning, we are encouraged to always be switched on. Simply being and observing is something unfamiliar and unrewarded in the production and consumption worldview, always on auto-pilot, always busy doing, without taking the time to simply be or reflect.

If we want to create a livable 21st century, it is imperative that we develop the practice of being with whatever shows up in life. We don't need to wait until we've worked through our emotions in Express. We can also start with Presence practices. If you haven't done any work in the Express domain, then the two will work well together. When you work in Presence, you might encounter material that is too energetic for you to simply be with. You might need to find ways to express the emotion, grounding it through, and then moving it out of your body.

Your inner-listening practice may take place sitting on a cushion or a chair with your eyes closed or gaze dropped. Or you may have a movement practice, for example, walking mindfully in nature, doing qigong, or dancing. I have a friend who connects with her inner voice while milking the goat.

The purpose of sitting on the cushion or walking or dancing is to become present, in the moment, in the now, letting thoughts of the future and thoughts of the past drop away. Through this regular practice, you will be able to stay present during those times when life is stormy and unsettling, giving you an opportunity to face your pain. You will be present enough to respond. Stilling the mind of chatter provides the opportunity to open up an inner space that is regenerative and life affirming. It is in these moments that insight as to right action drops in.

My invitation in *Life Design for Women* is to embrace this space—your inner space—and awaken both your "being" energy and your "doing" energy. Once you have created this connection with stillness, when you do act in the world, it will be from a place of being, of presence. You will find you won't have to push or force your action; the situation will unfold.

We all receive the invitation to be still and listen, and most of us ignore it. It happened to me when I was 13, while I was attending a weekly theater workshop. A visiting theater company had come to work with our group to put on a production, and one of the actors gave me a book on meditation by Alan Watts. I can't remember the title, but I can still see the cover. I delved into this mysterious world, but at the time it went completely over my head. Then, in my 20s, I met a shiatsu practitioner and felt prompted to study this energy healing method. As noted earlier, as part of my training, I was required to take up the practice of meditation. There are many other prompts and nudges I could recount, but I would like you to explore through reflection what prompts you experienced and either acted on or pushed aside.

When you bring Presence more fully into your life, be careful that you don't skip the work in the Express domain. Presence practices can be used to avoid feeling the sensations of your emotional pain; this is known as "spiritual bypass." You can't prevent or avoid strong emotions moving through you; you need to express them or transform them by being present with them. Doing nothing and pretending you are present with them is merely suppression in a different form. You won't find any benefit in this, and in the long term, you may even experience more physical and mental imbalances.

Practices that support you in developing Presence include mindfulness or heart-centered meditation and focused movement practices, such as slow walking meditation, perhaps in a labyrinth. You can practice a form of qigong or yoga. Singing or chanting and circle dancing are other practices that can help you connect.

- What inner listening practices have you experienced?
- What do you experience when you are still?
- What are you afraid you will discover by inner listening?
- Can you simply observe yourself when your emotions are triggered?
- Can you be and wait for a prompt for right action, or do you jump right in?

**OBSERVE YOUR PRESENT**

- Currently, I practice inner listening by . . .
- I don't have an inner listening practice yet, but I'm curious about . . .
- Until now I've avoided any inner listening practice because . . .
- What would support me to practice regularly is . . .

**REFLECT ON YOUR PAST**

- I used to think inner listening was . . .
- Inner listening never featured in my life because . . .
- The first time I ever got a prompt to practice inner listening was . . .
- Prompts to inner listening that I've ignored are . . .
- As a child, I learned that inner listening was . . .

**CONSIDER THE PLANET**

- The impact on nature and the planet from the way I live in my Presence domain is . . .

**CELEBRATE**

- Life-giving skills I have learned and developed in my Presence domain are . . .

If you are ready to continue with the **OREDA** design process for this domain, go to **Envision** on page 158.

## IMMERSE

As life-long learners, when we are in our Immerse domain we are actively developing our mind, specifically becoming aware of our thoughts and thought processes and how they help or hinder us in daily life. Our ability to think well about our being and doing with clarity and understanding will make life a more joyful experience.

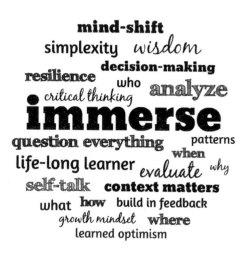

As life is precious, we want to be able to discern which situations are essential for us to put our time and attention into and take action on, and which are not. When we do engage in a particular activity, we want to become aware of our mindset. Are we fixed in our approach, or do we have an anything-is-possible attitude?

The latter approach, the growth mindset, is the approach we will naturally adopt as life-long learners. It's the approach we need to take in response to the current planetary crises. Top-performing athletes use the growth mindset, and mental health and well-being professionals increasingly embrace it.

Using a growth mindset as the basis of our Immerse domain, it is helpful to understand the underlying patterns in our thought processes. How do we identify our aims and decide how we will accomplish them? What information do we need to gather, and how do we make enough sense of it to make a decision? What happens to our thought process when unexpected events occur?

One process where we need to hone our skill is decision-making. Navigating life involves a constant process of making small and large decisions, and at times, we may be making more than one decision at a time, which can be confusing. There are several parts to a decision; in some cases, especially if the decision is one we're making for ourselves, it all can happen in an instant, so that you don't even notice the parts. Within a particular life domain or context, we identify a goal we want to aim for, make a proposal we think will move us toward our aim, respond by consenting or not consenting to the proposal, then the agreed action is taken. Then the next proposal arises, and so on.

We make some decisions so quickly we don't even notice that we've made a proposal to ourselves, or that the decision has taken place; we're already taking action on it. Behind every action lies a decision, whether it be getting out of bed in the morning or taking a new path in our career. Some choices are more complex, so we may need to gather more information, to both create the proposal and make the decision.

While working at IBM, David Snowden developed his model for making sense of the situations teams often faced when working. He called it a Cynefin (cu-nevin). He observed that in life, we face different decision-making contexts, which range from obvious to complicated, to complex, to chaotic, to disorder. It is essential to cultivate our skills in identifying which context we're in, and then bring the appropriate approach for thinking well in that context, both personally and professionally. Thinking skills that help us gain clarity are critical now, as we need to immerse ourselves in the chaotic and complex issues taking place on the planet and see how we can engage meaningfully in response. Often decisions are delayed because we haven't gathered enough information, and we waste our energy through this lack of clarity.

On a personal level, our thinking capacity can also get deployed in energy-wasting thoughts, leading to problems arising in our Embody and Express domains. We may worry endlessly about something happening in our life, rather than taking the time to think things through logically and making sure we have the right information available. Some of us avoid making decisions, or put time and energy into making small choices, as a way of putting off the crucial ones. When we focus on small decisions, rather than the big ones that have the potential to improve our lives, it may partly be due to the situation being a source of painful emotions for us. If we haven't done the work of processing feelings that are connected to the decision, through expressing or observing and transforming them, we are likely to avoid making the decision in order to avoid feeling the pain.

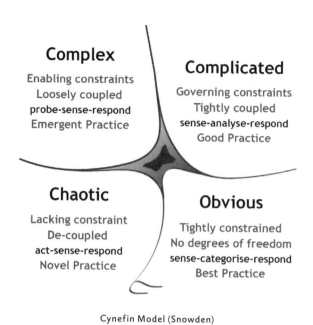

**Cynefin Model (Snowden)**

Until now the human collective has not been thinking well about what we're doing to the planet, our life-support system. We see what's happening, yet somehow most of us can't stop perpetuating behaviors that contribute to the devastation. As we deepen our understanding of what is occurring on the planet, honing our ability to clearly communicate our findings to others will be essential. People who want to maintain the status quo generally approach life mentally and logically, so we will need to use clear, rational thinking to meet them where they are comfortable and then demonstrate clearly and logically how we could do things differently.

We can play our part if we hone our Immerse domain by questioning everything and looking for underlying patterns in what we are being told, shown, or experiencing. Using frameworks like this Life Design can help you work through complexity. The Life Design framework supports you to think critically and creatively about your life and to question your choices and decide on a course of action. Another helpful framework used in critical thinking is the 5Ws+1H. The 5 Ws are *who? what? where? when? why?* and the H is *how?* You can apply this framework to formulate questions for any situation you want to understand more thoroughly.

- How engaged in your Immerse domain are you?
- In what ways do you stick to what you know?

- In what ways are you open to learning and feedback?
- What are the underlying processes you go through when you're making decisions?
- When do you find yourself confused about what is going on?
- In what ways do you think critically about your own life and why you do things the way you do them?
- In what ways do you think critically about events in your life?
- In what ways do you question why people say what they say and do what they do?
- In what situations do you simply accept people's words and deeds?
- How could you use your skills in your Immerse domain to make a regenerative contribution to life on Earth?

**OBSERVE YOUR PRESENT**

- The mindset I tend to approach life with is . . .
- When it comes to decision-making, I . . .
- Making decisions becomes difficult when . . .
- Critical thinking is something I . . .
- When faced with a complex situation, I . . .

**REFLECT ON YOUR PAST**

- As a child, the mindset I was encouraged to have was . . .
- In the past, decision-making was . . .
- The impact of putting off a life decision was . . .
- When it comes to critical thinking, I learned that . . .

**CONSIDER THE PLANET**

- The impact on nature and the planet from the way I live in my Immerse domain is . . .

**CELEBRATE**

- The mindset skills I have are . . .
- The decision-making skills I have are . . .
- The critical thinking skills I have are . . .

If you are ready to continue with the **OREDA** design process for this domain, go to **Envision** on page 158.

**PLAY**

The Play domain is about allowing time and space to have fun, play, and re-create ourselves. When we play, we do things that allow our imagination and spontaneity to come fully alive. There is an aspect of purposeful purposelessness to it. You purposefully drop out of your scheduled life and let things unfold. You let go and unwind. Play is the domain where we enjoy daydreaming and remembering, relaxing, and having fun. In this domain, it's possible to experience peace of mind.

There's something about the expansive space created by play, where you allow your body, spirit, soul, and mind to reset and refresh. It's a bit like the process of defragmenting your computer hard drive. Your consciousness gets the space it needs to work on the integration of all the associated experiences you've had, and through this, your life force is freed up. Through play, we bring to life aspects of our self that in other contexts may not get airtime. We discover latent parts of our personalities that may provide us with insights into other areas of life.

There are many ways to play, at different life stages, and we might have more than one form of play and do it either on our own or with friends. We can get together with others to play games, have parties, and enjoy dinners, or we can meander aimlessly through winding streets in an unexplored neighborhood of our city. Play is an essential domain.

Actively attending to your Play domain can be considered to be part of cultivating your Sovereign Self. Play offers a place where you can explore and experience more of your authenticity. This domain is not essential to living life—it is possible to get by without it—but do you want to just get by? I remember times in my life when I didn't attend to my Play domain; I was too focused on my work, and eventually I burned out.

In this domain, you have the opportunity to switch off and de-stress. Play is the domain that often gets neglected when we are younger and focused on our career or on raising a family. A healthy Play domain contributes to our mental well-being. Keeping our noses to the grindstone—whichever grindstone you've ended up with, and even if you love yours —will contribute to burnout. It's vital to switch off and unwind constructively. Slumping in front of the television or computer screen might feel good but could be a form of addiction. It's worth pausing to check in with yourself and make sure it's not your way of zoning out and numbing yourself.

Healthy play will regenerate your life force. Have you noticed how energized you feel after you've engaged in a physical game with your family or friends for an hour or so? This is regenerative recreation. Notice how you feel at the end of a session of zoning out in front of the TV. Designing activities in our Play domain that are both good for us and the planet is our Life Design challenge.

I love playing a game I call The Game. The process is simple and easy to follow, which makes the game accessible to people from all cultures. The group creates the "playing cards," so to speak, and then forms two teams. The process unfolds in rounds that involve different activities, including describing what's on the card without using the words on the card, acting the word out, drawing it, and finally distilling it down to one word.

The game is rooted in improvisation and spontaneity. I find that I discover parts of myself, playful or willing-to-be-silly, that don't otherwise get expressed. My friends get to reveal parts of themselves that I've never met before. Laughter becomes an inevitable component, as we find creative ways to communicate, and I notice a new-found deeper sense of connection through the simple shared experience.

Another way I play is by picking up trash. Several times a year, my friends and I would organize a trash pickup on the shores of the East River in the Bronx in New York City. While it is a purposeful activity, it is guided by the trash on the ground, so it has a meandering, playful quality to it. Bringing play into your life can be a small and simple act and it's possible to find ways to play that include caring for the planet.

- In what ways do you have Play designed into your life?
- What adjustments could you make so that it's fun for you and the planet?
- Is the way you play the way you've always done it with your family or with friends?
- Is shopping for things your current form of Play? What else could you do that invokes similar feelings, but doesn't involve acquiring more stuff?
- Is the way you play really nurturing and revitalizing you? Is it authentic?
- In what ways are you just following the crowd?
- Have you found play activities that are right for you?

**OBSERVE YOUR PRESENT**

- I make time for the Play domain by . . .
- Being unscheduled and relaxed makes me . . .
- The ways I like to play and have fun are . . .
- Play is something that I . . .

**REFLECT ON YOUR PAST**

- As a child, I experienced play as . . .
- I learned that relaxing and being purposeless was . . .

**CONSIDER THE PLANET**

- The impact on nature and the planet from the way I live in my Play domain is . . .

**CELEBRATE**

- Life-giving skills I have learned and developed in my Play domain are . . .

If you are ready to continue with the **OREDA** design process for this domain, go to **Envision** on page 158.

### CREATE

The Create domain is about tapping into your imagination, inventiveness, and curiosity and combining this with your skills in a particular area to invent, build, design, compose, or interpret. You bring elements from the same field or diverse fields together with the aim of accomplishing something new. You might have a particular objective in mind, or you might follow the process to see what emerges.

We are all capable of creativity. Creativity occurs when two or more seemingly unconnected ideas or elements are combined to create something new. In our daily life we have the potential to create all the time—combining different foods in a tasty dish, arranging clothing for a new or unique look, or organizing our day so that we work more effectively. Now we need to dig deeper and find more impactful ways of applying our creativity to the planetary challenges we face.

Creativity is often associated with the arts, but other fields also engage creativity. It is increasingly recognized as one of the top transferable skills in the workplace. Now more than ever, the world needs you to direct your creativity toward rethinking and redesigning the countless and complex ways in which we humans currently meet our needs. Discernment is a critical partner to our creativity. Is the solution we create contributing to a regenerative future or will it take us on the same life-diminishing trajectory?

If you don't think you can find that kind of creativity in you, think again. As a consumer you have experience with the things you buy—for example, how well they do the job you bought them for, how easy they are to operate; you can also start to consider what impact they are having on the planet.

You are part of what is usually a linear production process: design, produce, distribute, purchase, use/consume, trash. You usually enter the process at the point of purchase, you use or consume the item, and at some point, you trash it. By applying your creativity, you could take any item that you need or want in life and find out how it could be produced in a more regenerative, life-affirming way. Looking for circular solutions is an excellent place to start. How could the same thing be made in a way that has minimal damaging impact on the environment, or even better, how could it be produced in a way that supports regeneration of natural systems as part of the process?

By letting this domain lie dormant, we lose a unique opportunity to discover more of who we are, who our Sovereign Self is, and how she authentically expresses herself. Create is the domain that calls you forth to play a bigger game. Embracing your deep well of creativity will draw out more parts of yourself. You'll apply the skills, experience, and knowledge you have, and discover more as you create.

If we don't activate Create and begin to apply our individual and collective brilliance to find life-supporting ways to meet our human needs, there won't be a planet fit for any life. There's a tremendous job to do, and women need to show up and get on with it. History is full of women inventors, some of whom had no technical or engineering training. The windscreen wiper, the first solar-powered home, and the circular saw were all invented by women.

During World War II, government propaganda mobilized women to do their part. I've heard interviews of women recounting how they felt a great sense of liberation and came alive when they took on roles traditionally held by men, who were away fighting in the war. Suddenly these women were discovering and tapping into more of their creativity and capacity.

I found an inspiring example of such a woman. At the start of the Second World War, the famous 1940s Hollywood actress Hedy Lamarr was already a silver screen success. Originally from Austria, she was determined to do her bit in the war effort. She collaborated on the invention of a radio guidance system for Allied torpedoes. While not used at the time, the US Navy did eventually put it to use in the 1960s. Today, we benefit from her invention, as it forms the basis of Bluetooth technology.

Globally, we are facing challenges that need that same level of mobilization and sacrifice as there was during World War II. This time it's not a war we're fighting but our collective apathy. We all need to break free from the grip of consumer culture and start creating a way of life that ensures the necessary social foundations for all humans while remaining within the planetary boundaries. We need creative responses that support us to live within the safe-operating space of Doughnut Economics. By activating your life force in the Create domain, you have the potential to discover more of who you are and what you are capable of, and to make a life-affirming contribution.

- What's alive in your Create domain?
- What have you created in your life?
- Have you ever invented something?
- Do you play a small game with your creativity?
- How could you play a bigger game?
- Is there an aspect of nature that calls to your creativity for help?
- Is your creativity-for-the-sake-of-life relegated to the sidelines while you pursue personal gain?
- What could you set up, construct, build, invent, or initiate as a contribution to our thriving future?

**OBSERVE YOUR PRESENT**

- I tap into my creativity by . . .
- My Create domain is . . .
- The challenges I experience with my creativity are . . .
- The situations in which I find myself most creative are . . .

**REFLECT ON YOUR PAST**

- As a child, my creativity was . . .
- I learned that creativity was . . .
- I used my creativity to . . .

**CONSIDER THE PLANET**

- The impact on nature and the planet from the way I live in my Create domain is . . .

**CELEBRATE**

- Life-giving skills I have learned and developed in my Create domain are . . .

If you are ready to continue with the **OREDA** design process for this domain, go to **Envision** on page 158.

## ADORN

Our Adorn domain contains the elements of Life Design that relate to how we clothe ourselves, including the accessories, makeup, and other beauty products we use. I've chosen to call the domain Adorn as I wanted to use this delicious word, which invokes sumptuousness and goddess-like qualities. Adorning oneself is more than merely putting on clothing; it's an invitation to seek out your own unique expression through clothing and accessories. It's a beautiful way to demonstrate who you are and can bring a great deal of enjoyment.

Today, adornment is a multi-trillion-dollar global industry aimed at women and increasingly, men. Clothes are no longer used merely to protect our body, keep us warm in cold climates, or shield us from the sun in hot climates. The clothing industry is vast, but along with the fun and enjoyment of fashion, it also affects Earth in life-diminishing ways through its manufacturing processes.

Through the concept of fashion, the clothing industry has created built-in obsolescence and perpetual need in two primary ways. The first is that the fabrics used to make clothing don't last as long as they once did, so the garment wears out or looks shabby sooner. The second is that the industry plays on our tendency to generate negative thoughts about ourselves by overwhelming us with images of how we should look and then leaving it to us to measure ourselves against these ideals. As a result of our unhappiness with the way we look, we become consumers of "fast fashion" by discarding astounding quantities of perfectly good clothing.

According to Clare Farrell, a UK fashion designer and environmental activist, "global clothing consumption has doubled in the past 15 years, while utilization—how often clothes are worn—has decreased by 36 percent, with total greenhouse gas emissions from textile production at 1.2 billion tons annually, exceeding those of all international flights and maritime shipping combined."

In a scene in *Hugh's War on Waste*, a 2015 BBC television program in the United Kingdom, the show's presenter, Hugh Fearnley-Whittingstall, climbed onto a huge, seven-ton pile of 10,000 pieces of clothing. The pile represented the amount of clothing the country throws out in 10 minutes. If that clothes hill represents the United Kingdom, which has a population of about 66 million people, what would the pile be like if this visual was recreated in the United States, which has a population of 300 million and a much stronger throw-away ethic? Energy and other resources go into making our clothing. Every time we throw an item away, we are wasting these mostly nonrenewable resources and energy.

The fashion industry also takes its toll on the workers, most of whom are women, who have to work in abusive and harsh conditions under high production pressures. They sit behind sewing machines, wearing protective masks, churning out hundreds of items of clothing every day. Garment workers are often subject to obligatory overtime, with no way to refuse.

Something else to consider in relation to planetary well-being when you adorn yourself is the material used to make the clothing. Where plant-based fabrics are used, how are the plants that are used to make the fabrics grown? A tremendous amount of water and chemicals is used in cotton production, for example. Chemically produced synthetic fabrics, such as acrylic, nylon, and polyester, are made from non-biodegradable plastics. The problem with these fabrics is that when you wash them, they release millions of particles of microplastics into our water systems and thence, our oceans, destroying the habitat for all marine species. Clothing made with sustainably grown natural fibers, such as hemp, bamboo, linen, and wool, will help your life force to flow through your body.

Jewelry can add a striking, head-turning touch to what we're wearing. I'm amazed by the quantity of jewelry made. I remember walking through Chatuchak Market in Bangkok, past rows of tables displaying thousands of semi-precious stones. I was overwhelmed by their sheer quantity, and found myself wondering how it could be that so many precious and semi-precious stones are mined from the earth. How could there be that many? Then I found myself hoping that, for the sake of the planet, most of these stones were fakes. Then again, fake jewelry is not a better option, as it is made from plastics that, once discarded, will adorn the surface of Earth in landfills for decades. Giving thought to how we can accessorize in a way that is caring for the planet is part of the process of thoughtful adornment.

What about beauty products? Many beauty products, including makeup and designer perfumes, are made with chemicals and chemically manufactured scent. When you put these products on your skin, your body absorbs them, and over time they accumulate, potentially having a detrimental effect on your health. When your sense of smell becomes more sensitive through eating healthfully and through physical activity, you may find the intense smell of these products becomes unpleasant. If you start to use healthy beauty products, you'll find that they are either fragrance-free, or if they are scented, the perfume comes from essential oils naturally extracted from plants.

Where to start on the life-affirming path of adornment? The first step is to do the inner work, to detach what you wear and your external appearance from your inner power, the power to be able to influence your surroundings, your sovereign power. Doing inner work will help you disconnect from measuring yourself against others, whether that's people around you or the images from the fashion and beauty industries. As part of this inner work, reflect on what feeling you are seeking when you buy more clothes or jewelry. If you don't need them, are you just fulfilling a desire?

Then there are the practical steps of assessing your wardrobe and everything you use in this domain. What do you already have? What do you need? Where will you get it? The Japanese decluttering expert Marie Kondo is having an impact worldwide with her approach to organization, specifically, her use of a concept she calls Spark Joy. She invites people to make an assessment of each item of clothing in their wardrobe, as well as other items they want to clean out, and to keep what "sparks joy" and lovingly pass on anything they no longer want.

When you do need more clothes, other items for your adornment, or just to exercise your desire to shop, you have a whole range of more life-affirming options than buying new to choose from.

For example, you can go "thrifting" and buy reasonably priced, gently used pre-loved clothing from thrift stores, or check out higher-priced consignment and vintage shops and online options, such as eBay and Etsy. Making it a priority to purchase pre-loved clothing is a significant step toward doing your part for the planet. What I love about shopping for preowned clothing is that I never know what I'm going to find, and often I return from a shopping trip with something I love and wear frequently.

A fun way to find clothing and accessories is to hold a clothes swap party. Invite your friends to bring over any clothes they're bored with, place them in a big pile, then everyone can have fun trying things on, changing their wardrobe for free, and receive supportive feedback about how great they look. The bonus with this event is you get to enjoy time with friends.

When it comes to beauty products, where possible choose products made from organically grown plants, as these are products that are genuinely natural. Some brands put the word "natural" on their products as a way of selling something that doesn't have anything remotely natural in it. Genuinely organic and regeneratively grown materials may cost more, but in the long run they're better for your health.

When it comes to my Adorn domain, I'm not perfect, and I do have compromises in my wardrobe. As much as possible, I buy clothing made with natural fibers, but living in a cooler climate and easily feeling the cold, I do have a warm puffy jacket with synthetic filling, which I often wear, even in the summer at times.

The point is that it is possible to develop an awareness of how we adorn ourselves. We can recognize that the drive for adornment in all its forms is fueled by image makers whose job it is to make us feel unhappy and unsatisfied with our appearance. Our natural beauty is unique to us and doesn't have to fit their stereotypes.

- Are you constantly unhappy with your appearance?
- What beliefs do you have about how you should look?
- Do you buy more clothing than you actually wear?
- Do you know what you have in your wardrobe?
- Do you feel overwhelmed by the amount of clothing you have?
- Is your bathroom cluttered with bottles and containers of beauty products?
- Do you have shoes and bags you haven't used in a year sitting in your closet or stashed in another part of the house?

**OBSERVE YOUR PRESENT**

- Beliefs I have about how to adorn myself are . . .
- What I love about the Adorn domain is . . .
- What I find challenging about the Adorn domain is . . .

**REFLECT ON YOUR PAST**

- As a child, I learned that the way I adorned myself is . . .
- The messages I received about my clothing were . . .

**CONSIDER THE PLANET**

- The impact on nature and the planet from the way I live in my Adorn domain is . . .

**CELEBRATE**

- Life-giving skills I have learned and developed in my Adorn domain are . . .

If you are ready to continue with the **OREDA** design process for this domain, go to **Envision** on page 158.

## HOMESTEAD REALM

A homestead usually refers to a house on land that is farmed. In this section, I'm using the word "homestead" as a way of grouping into a single realm all the parts that make up your home: your house and furnishings, all your stuff, digital devices, transport, and if you have it, land. Our Homestead realm is where we can look at our ecological footprint to assess the impact our lifestyle has on the planet.

Your ecological footprint is the demand your lifestyle makes on natural resources to meet your needs. The footprint is measured in the number of "planet Earths" needed if everyone lived the way you do. For example, if everyone lived the way the average person in the United States lives, we'd need five Earths to keep that lifestyle going. The problem is that we only have one Earth. The ecological footprint shows us the actions we can take to reduce our footprint. To find out what your ecological footprint is you can use the Global Footprint Network's online calculator. You'll find out how many planets your lifestyle requires by responding to a few questions about your food, travel, housing, and energy choices.

Nestled within the ecological footprint are calculations for your carbon footprint. This is the measurement of how much carbon dioxide, a climate change greenhouse gas, your lifestyle generates. The carbon measurement converts the other greenhouse gases into a carbon equivalent, so those gases are factored in too.

Our homestead, whatever its size, is the element in our life where we use an enormous amount of energy, not only our life force but also energy from other greenhouse gas-emitting sources. We use our life force to operate and maintain everything in our homestead. We use energy to heat and cool the rooms, power electronic devices, lights, and other appliances, and to heat water. This energy comes from a range of sources, both renewable and nonrenewable. How much life force we use will depend on how much help we get from our energy-powered electronic devices and other appliances, and how organized we are.

Energy is the generator of our lives. It takes energy to get more energy, so finding ways to preserve energy, or use less of it, means that we don't have to work so hard to get it in the first place. As we become more energy-savvy, we learn how to stop wasting energy, both our life force and fuel, by using it wisely.

In 2014 environmentalist Paul Hawken founded Project Drawdown. The purpose of this project is to identify, research, and rank the most effective solutions we could apply individually and collectively that would have a beneficial impact on the planet. The first item on the list is refrigerant management: Our refrigerators and air conditioners use chemicals called HFCs, which, while they don't damage the delicate ozone layer that surrounds the planet, do have a vastly higher capacity than carbon dioxide to warm the atmosphere. Fortunately, in 2016, 170 countries agreed on a solution that involves the phasing out of these harmful chemicals.

Other items on the list that relate to our Homestead include district heating (no. 27), solar rooftops (no. 10), water-saving (no. 46), ride-sharing (no. 75). Some of these solutions, like saving water, we can apply individually through changing our water-use habits; or ride-sharing where we can offer lifts to neighbors and work colleagues who are traveling to and from nearby destinations. Others like district heating require a collective approach, probably with the support of our local governments. Some solutions like solar rooftops may be out of reach in terms of cost for many of us. Governments can support this solution by providing grants and incentives that reduce the upfront costs of installing the solar panels. Once installed, people who live in homes with solar panels are delighted to see their energy bills decrease.

Working with the Life Design process will give you the opportunity to get clear on what you could change to preserve energy or use less of it in your Homestead domains. You might discover that you merely need to turn your thermostat down a few degrees or tidy up more frequently, or that a computer skills course could help you reduce how much life force you lose in frustration, wading through tech glitches.

## HOME

The domain of Home is an invitation for you to have a closer look at your house and how you make it into a home through the way you live in it. Your furniture, furnishings, and large appliances are included in this domain.

As you're doing this Life Design process, I assume you are fortunate enough to have a home or some kind of shelter. There's a range of options for shelter, some of them include a house, a duplex, a row house, a tiny house, an apartment or condo, a loft or studio, a mobile home, an RV, or a houseboat or canal barge. Each of these has an ecological and a carbon footprint, which will be large or small, depending on what it is and how you live in it. Whatever its shape and size, your home provides you with a place to carry out all of your Well-Being and other activities. It keeps you dry and warm, or cool, and provides you with air and water. You enjoy a sense of safety and belonging living there.

Our shelter becomes a home through the way we pour our unique expression into it. It can be a regenerative place or one that sucks the life out of you. Through observation, I've noticed that women have a tendency to feather their nests through the accumulation of things. Unlike birds, which make a new nest each year, we tend to keep the same one and fill it up with more stuff. Is this because traditionally and up until recently, being the home-maker, we've been targeted through advertising to accumulate things?

A house is a complex entity. It consists of many systems designed to fulfill our needs, wants, and desires. Each system requires inputs in order to function, usually in the form of energy; through use, inputs are transformed, and by that process, create outputs. The conventional ways that systems work in a house are linear, with the outputs typically including some form of waste. For example, doing the laundry, the inputs are your dirty clothes, detergent, and clean water, and the outputs are your clean wet clothes and the dirty water going down the drain.

Through Life Design, we apply circulating design thinking to look for ways to minimize the waste we generate in our homes. We take an ecological systems approach by asking where the inputs come from and what happens to the outputs when we're done with them. We then look to see if we could redesign the system and use the outputs in other ways. In the laundry example, instead of allowing the wastewater to disappear into the sewer system, it could be filtered through a simple plant-based purification system and used again time as graywater to water trees in the garden. In water-starved desert communities, such as Phoenix, Arizona, this is already happening on a large scale as part of citywide reclaimed water programs, as well as encouraged at the household level.

With so much complexity, a healthy home needs to be consciously and lovingly designed. We need to have a dynamic relationship with it. If we take the time to do this, the way we live in our home can contribute to the regeneration of the planet as well as our own well-being. The main areas we will explore in Home are energy, temperature, air quality, water and waste, and how we use the space. Our homes are the scene of our waste crimes, and we get away with murder. Homes are wasteful, especially if their design is based on linear and particle thinking. We waste a great deal of energy in our homes through poor heating and cooling systems, leaving lights on, and running older appliances. Drinkable water flows down the drain when we brush our teeth, and when we use it to flush our toilets. We bring thousands of items into our homes, and when we're done with them, we chuck them out. We bring most of those items into our homes wrapped in single-use packaging, plastic, paper, or cardboard. We throw out food that we let go moldy in the fridge or past its use-by date, and it ends up in a landfill or being incinerated.

To meet our needs, we run an enormous amount of energy through our homes. Until recently, the energy has mainly come from nonrenewable fossil fuel sources: oil, gas, and coal. Once we've used up these energy sources, there aren't any more. New discoveries of nonrenewable fuels are slowing down, involve blasting the tops off mountains, or are in designated nature reserves and other precious protected public lands.

Our lives have been hardwired for using nonrenewable fossil fuels, and apart from the fact that these fossil fuels will run out, when we use them, they emit greenhouse gases, the primary cause of the changing climate. The largest amount of energy is used to control the temperature of our homes, to heat or cool them. We also use energy to operate all of our electronic devices, lighting, and appliances, and for heating water.

We overuse water, some of which has to do with our unconscious use of it, and some as a result of the appliances we use. It's lovely to stand under that warm, flowing water after a challenging day and so tempting to linger a little longer. Fortunately, some innovations help us reduce our water consumption. If your home or appliances are old, they will probably have missed the shift in water conservation design and will use more energy and water than the new models. If you live in an older home, you might find that your toilet tank, for example, uses six gallons of water per flush on average, whereas new toilets use only about two gallons.

Many of us live in houses that have more rooms than we actually need. There are large bedrooms that are empty the whole day and en-suite bathrooms that are only ever used at the beginning and the end of the day. There's a tendency for oversized houses to become expensive storage spaces for all the stuff we accumulate during our lives. If the house isn't big enough, some of us even pay rent to keep our stuff in a storage facility.

The other way we waste our life force is by living in a cluttered, disorganized home. The consequence of living this way is that we spend countless hours looking for the things we need. The art of life is being able to do what we need and want with the minimal amount of time hunting for things. It's possible to store everything in your home in such a way that you can easily find and use it. This doesn't mean that everything needs to be arranged in a sterile, unimaginative way. It is possible to organize your home in a way that gives you pleasure while optimizing your energy use.

In addition to the wasteful aspects of life in your home, it is also worth looking at the quality of your indoor air, as it can support or undermine your health. There are many sources of air pollution in your home. These include fuel-burning combustion appliances, such as a gas boiler; products used for household cleaning and maintenance, personal care, and hobbies; excess moisture, leading to the development of mold; smoke from tobacco products; toxic building materials; off gassing furnishings; and outdoor sources of pollution, such as pesticides and general pollution. Being aware of this and taking action can lead to improvements in your Well-Being domains.

- What kind of relationship do you have with your home?
- Where do the inputs for your home come from?
- Where do the outputs (waste) from your home go?
- What do you waste?
- What could you do to use less water?
- Where does your home's energy come from?
- What underlying unconscious patterns influence the way you live in your home?
- What agreements have you made with the people you share your home with about where things are stored?
- What are the essential items you need to run and maintain your home?
- What do you consciously choose to bring into your home?
- What things do you frequently throw out, discard, or waste that could be used in other ways?

**OBSERVE YOUR PRESENT**

- The relationship I have with my house is . . .
- I make my house a home by . . .
- The ways I'm wasteful in my home are . . . (consider the areas I mentioned above)
- The air quality in my home is . . .
- The inputs needed for my house to function optimally are . . .

**REFLECT ON YOUR PAST**

- As a child, I learned that my home was . . .
- As a child, waste was . . .
- I thought energy was . . .
- I thought waste was . . .

**CONSIDER THE PLANET**

- The impact on nature and the planet from the way I live in my Home domain is . . .

**CELEBRATE**

- Life-giving skills I have learned and developed in my Home domain are . . .

If you are ready to continue with the **OREDA** design process for this domain, go to **Envision** on page 158.

## STUFF

Stuff is where you bring your focus to equipment, paraphernalia, tools, supplies, paperwork, and bits and pieces—in short, all the stuff you have in your home. Here you have the opportunity to explore your relationship with them and recover the energy you expend to maintain, store, and operate them.

recycle
story your stuff
share gift clear out
reuse borrow
tidy **stuff** declutter
is it needed? gives pleasure organized
peace of mind minimalist
gratitude reduce use or pass on
gift experiences repair
a place for everything
story of stuff
donate

We've absorbed the message perpetuated through consumer culture that we will be happy if we accumulate more and more stuff. In this way, though, we end up with so many things we start to experience overwhelm, or we shove them into the spare room or garage, so they are out of sight. We forget what we have and buy more, even if we don't really need it. Then we go into shock when we discover that we're living in a house that's piled high with stuff.

Every single item in your possession, even if you don't think about it or interact with it every day, holds a tiny bit of your life force. By sifting through and reducing your belongings to what is essential in your life, you can recover a tremendous amount of your life force. By choosing not to bring it into your life in the first place, you will conserve an immense amount of personal energy. Think about all the time and effort you put into acquiring the stuff, storing it, maintaining it, and feeling sorry that you aren't looking after it.

Some of us engage in collecting particular items, and our homes become crammed with them. It may be that these are collector's items with some monetary value, or simply give you pleasure, but is this worth more than being able to live in a home you can fully enjoy? Is living with hundreds of pairs of shoes, or plastic dolls in their original packaging, or pig-shaped decorations truly enhancing your quality of life?

Even if you have your stuff all neatly organized, you might still have much more than you need. Equipment for hobbies or sports no longer pursued is stashed, perhaps with the hope that at some point you will return to it; meanwhile, it is gathering dust and might even become moldy. At some point, all you can do is put it in the trash, but if you had gotten to it sooner, you could have put it into circulation so that someone else could use it.

There is a fine art to passing things on. You might come back to the hobby or sport, either because you have the time again or you realize how important that activity was in your life, and find that you do need the item. If the equipment enables you to do something you love, and is irreplaceable, then it might be something worth keeping for a few more months, to see if you make the time to take up that activity again. The other art in passing things on is that you don't keep the item so long that it is no longer usable, either because the material has broken down or the item is out of date.

Establishing some kind of personal guideline on how you want to deal with your stuff can help with the decision-making process when you want to move things on. Some people decide on a length of time they will keep an item they aren't using. If in six months they haven't used it, the piece is put into storage, and if around a year later they still haven't used it, they pass it on. Another approach, usually employed once people have pared down to just what's needed, is the policy of one item in, one item out. If they want to buy something, then something has to go. If you still have a lot of things you need to release, you could play around with this, for example try one thing in, five things out.

For some of us, it's difficult to discern what is worth keeping and what needs to be discarded. It's especially hard when the stuff reminds us of a particular time in our lives. Perhaps we have kept letters from old lovers, or we have a baseball collection that our child gathered. The item becomes infused with our attachment to an experience or a person, and getting rid of it becomes fraught with emotion. It might be that we keep stuff around from a particularly painful time in our lives, and it's as if everything is frozen in time, both our emotions and our stuff. If you are willing to work courageously in this domain, it could have a beneficial impact on your Well-Being domains, particularly Express and Embody.

Then, of course, there are the family heirlooms we dutifully keep. Some mementos and precious items are worth keeping; learning to discern which ones, helps in decluttering. A wedding ring used over 10 generations might be worth handing down. If all the marriages in which the ring was used to tie the knot have ended in divorce or unhappiness, however, then perhaps this might not be something to burden the next generation with. If you are going to keep family heirlooms, you must be willing to become their curator. If there aren't any stories attached to an item, and nobody knows to whom it belonged, why would they care for it? Certain items were traditionally passed down because at one time those things cost a lot to acquire. Years ago, watches were costly and rare. It was common for people to pass them on to the next generation, as they were both useful and often came into the family through the hard work of a parent or grandparent.

Being overwhelmed by your stuff means that you have less attention available to give to the big issues we really need to be concerning ourselves with now. If we continue to accumulate items that block the flow in our homes, both physically and energetically, we perpetuate the systems that cause harm to our life-support systems. Earth has a limited capacity, both in terms of planetary boundaries and resources. If we continue to consume at the rate we have until now, and store more of it, turning it into junk or trashing it, then we are depleting precious nonrenewable resources.

Some companies are exploring making materials out of plants rather than nonrenewable fossil fuels. Lego, for example, is looking into making some of their building blocks from bioplastics; that is, plastics made from plants. The challenge is that we can't afford to take up precious food-producing land to grow the plants for making stuff. Perhaps we could make things out of byproducts. This practice is not something new. In countries where palm trees grow, people make baskets out of the branches that fall to the ground. This disappearing art is a good skill to preserve for the future.

Having a place and a use for everything is a high-level intervention that will bring energy flowing back into your life. You might already experience the benefits of having an organized home with a place for everything. It might well be that you are still holding on to too much. If you have too much stuff, and you haven't used much of it in years, you will quickly discover what needs to go and how much you should keep. This work requires time and commitment. It is well worth it. You will find that your life transforms as a result of attending to your stuff.

- What is essential for you to keep?
- Why do you save particular things?
- In what ways are you overwhelmed by your stuff?
- What could you do with your stuff to start making beneficial changes in your life?
- What equipment have you got stored away in the hope you'll return to the activity it was once used for?
- How does the stuff you keep support you in Well-Being or other domains of your life?
- How does the stuff you keep occupy your thoughts with the worry of what to do with it?
- Which rooms in your home have you shut the door to hoping the clutter will magically disappear?
- What are you holding onto that represents a particular time in your life that you are afraid to let go of?

**OBSERVE YOUR PRESENT**

- My relationship with my stuff is . . .
- The affirming ways my life is impacted by my stuff are . . .
- The diminishing ways my life is impacted by my stuff are . . .
- The way I care for my stuff is by . . .
- What I struggle with in relation to my stuff is . . .

**REFLECT ON YOUR PAST**

- As a child, I learned that stuff was . . .
- In my more recent past, stuff has . . .

**CONSIDER THE PLANET**

- The impact on nature and the planet from the way I live in my Stuff domain is . . .

**CELEBRATE**

- Life-giving skills I have learned and developed in my Stuff domain are . . .

If you are ready to continue with the **OREDA** design process for this domain, go to **Envision** on page 158.

## DIGITAL

The part of your life we will focus on in the Digital domain is everything to do with your digital life. When you think of your Digital domain, primarily consider how you use your devices. We're looking for the ways you interact with your Digital domain that make your life better and the ways that frustrate you or bog you down, unable to actually do what you wanted to do when you turned on the device.

The Digital realm has transformed our lives exponentially. This gadget revolution started in the 1990s with the development of laptops, followed by smartphones and tablets in the 2000s and 2010s, respectively. The innovations are constant. There are tiny computers inside many of the household gadgets we use. By combining computers, Bluetooth, and Wi-Fi, it's possible to create an automated house. As artificial intelligence (AI) develops, there will be even further innovations. Discernment is an important skill to apply to this domain.

On the face of it, technology has enhanced our lives a thousandfold in our work and personal life on a daily basis. The internet is mind-blowing! We are able to send a message to someone on the other side of the world who will receive it instantly. Brilliant human minds conceived and created this, along with all the other technological developments.

The price for these innovations is high, as hours and hours of our precious lives outside of work disappear into the Digital domain. Most of us are constantly plugged in and available, yet unavailable to our loved ones sitting right next to us. Sometimes I think that when the internet was invented, they should have found a way to add four more hours to the day just so that we have time to catch up on responding to emails and other digital communication.

It is important to be honest with yourself. Examine how much of your time you spend on your devices, and what you are actually doing. You could be investing your time well, using it to stay connected with family and friends who don't live close to you. You might have to be online for work. You might also be frittering away those minutes and hours and days, surfing social media or online shopping. Perhaps you engage in research on a topic that interests you, only to realize that you haven't documented it and forgot the key points within minutes of walking away from the computer. You might be escaping into the Digital domain to avoid painful emotions or a difficult situation with a loved one.

Practically, it could be that you lose time because you don't know how to use the device optimally, either the software or the hardware. Then there's the time spent if the device doesn't work and you start to tinker or surf the web to find a solution to the problem. Hours later, you still aren't any closer to solving it, and you are boiling with frustration as you work through the problem with the helpful person from the tech support team.

Digital Minimalism is a movement that is emerging as a response to this loss of quality of life. Cal Newport writes on how to design a better relationship with your digital life in his book, *Digital Minimalism*. He instigated the idea of undertaking a 30-day digital detox process whereby you stop using your gadgets and do other things with your precious time.

What about the fraudsters contacting you to let you know you've been hacked and promptly get you to share your screen and worse, your bank details with them. If this hasn't happened to you, you probably know of someone to whom it did.

If you've followed the crowd and gone wireless, using either Wi-Fi or Bluetooth technology, or mobile data through your smartphone, you expose yourself to health risks from the radiation caused by their electromagnetic fields (EMFs), and with the rollout of blanket coverage with 5G that's only going to become worse. Some people don't seem to be affected by EMF radiation; others suffer terribly, having to live in places on the planet where there are no EMFs, if possible, or insulate their homes or a room in their house with aluminum foil to protect themselves. It's a controversial issue, because it's in the interests of so many companies that we embrace this wireless life. For us, being wireless makes life easy and gives us a sense of freedom and access to information and games that potentially improve our quality of life.

The problem facing the planet when it comes to the Digital domain is that we become entirely disembodied and disconnected. For many people, their digital life is better than reality. When we favor a disembodied experience, how can we possibly care for the real world that surrounds us? We exist so much in the virtual world that we don't see what's happening to nature and her systems.

One thing we often fail to consider is the life-threatening experiences of the workers, in many cases children, who extract the minerals and metals used to manufacture our devices. Every day, there's a chance that they may lose their lives due to inadequate safety and health protection measures or abuse from the guards in the mines they work in. For working in these conditions they are paid a pittance, nothing close to a living wage. People who are involved in assembling the gadgets also suffer from physical and mental health issues.

Electronic waste is another challenge we face. The discarded devices pile up, as each year we are enticed to get the latest model. Some of us may be savvy enough to sell the item online for a discounted price and recoup some of our money, but ultimately, there is an end of the line for the gadget, and it will end up in an electronic waste pile. Recovering and recycling the materials in trashed smartphones and tablets is left to people who do it by hand under terrible working conditions without health protection. The work is harder and more hazardous, because manufacturers glue the components inside together.

- In what ways do you feel confident in your Digital domain?
- How often are you surfing online? If you are, what impact does this have on your energy?
- How dependent are you on your digital devices for feeling connected?
- How does being online all the time affect your relationships?
- How frequently do you upgrade to a new device?
- What do you do to extend your device's life?
- What happens to your energy when you are sucked into the frustration of not knowing how to get the results you were aiming for?

**OBSERVE YOUR PRESENT**

- When it comes to the Digital domain, I . . .
- The life-affirming aspects of my relationship with the Digital domain are . . .
- The degenerative aspects of my relationship with the Digital domain are . . .

**REFLECT ON YOUR PAST**

- As a child, the Digital domain was . . .
- I found positive Digital domain role models by . . .

**CONSIDER THE PLANET**

- The impact on nature and the planet from the way I live in my Digital domain is . . .

**CELEBRATE**

- Life-giving skills I have learned and developed in my Digital domain are . . .

If you are ready to continue with the **OREDA** design process for this domain, go to **Envision** on page 158.

## TRANSPORT

The Transport domain is all about the modes of transport you use to get you from home to work or other places. We will explore your transport choices and how you use them.

hydrogen fuel-cell
staycation  no fly zone
ecological footprint  walk
redesign infrastructure
**transport**
carpool
carbon footprint  electric car
fewer trips  train  bus
cycle  reduce miles
virtual commute
work locally

We have become heavily dependent on using cars, often one car per person. This is especially the case if we live in rural, suburban, or urban sprawl areas that are not well served, if at all, by public transport. We need to be able to get from home to work, school, or other places; a car or places, and a car is seen as the most convenient way to do that.

The problem with using private cars is that they require a lot of energy to run and until recently have mostly been fueled by gas and diesel. These fossil fuel-driven vehicles make a significant contribution to environmental damage, including climate change and air pollution. According to the United States Environmental Protection Agency (EPA), 28 percent of the country's greenhouse gases come from the transport sector, and when that figure is broken down, we find that 60 percent of those emissions come from the use of private cars.

Governments in nine countries have pledged to move entirely to zero-emission vehicles in the future. Sweden, for example, has pledged to have 100 percent zero-emission cars by 2025, and the United Kingdom has pledged the same by 2040. There is no support for a move to zero-emission transport in the United States, but some people are taking responsibility themselves and are making zero-emission choices by purchasing electric cars.

Owning your own car will cost you anywhere between 10 percent and 30 percent of your annual income, for car loan payments (if necessary), road tax (vehicle registration), insurance, fuel, and repairs and maintenance. Along with these costs, driving everywhere is also bad for our health as we become increasingly sedentary.

What about using other forms of transport? In the United States, the subtle message is that any kind of transport other than driving your own car is for poor people; whether it be walking, cycling, or taking public transport, the infrastructure discourages these forms of transportation in areas outside (and often within) cities. At a time when the future is at stake, we really need to become more nuanced in our approach to transport and look for ways to leave the car at home. Options include carpooling; free or low-cost shuttles, trams, and light rail; or, for shorter distances, health permitting, walking or cycling.

Walking or cycling builds exercise into our daily routine. If you live in the city, there are lots of opportunities for cycling and walking, and perhaps you're lucky enough to have an excellent public transport system. In cities like New York, cycling and walking are being encouraged with the installation of a network of cycling and walking paths. In Scotland, the Scottish government has funded an Active Travel initiative to get more people to cycle or walk to their destinations.

There may be a carshare scheme like Zip Car in your area. With this approach, you have the option to book different cars for different needs. Zip Car started a few years before I moved from New York. It was handy for work projects that involved hauling materials or scouting locations; I could hire the right car for each job.

Where I live now, I am a member of a carshare scheme. What I love about this is that the manager takes care of the car purchases, getting a good deal on insurance, and the cleaning and maintenance, all of this in return for a monthly membership fee and charges per mile and per hour. The cost for the membership is much less than having a car I infrequently drive parked outside the house.

- What types of transport are you dependent on?
- In what ways does your choice of transport contribute to environmental damage?
- What is it about where you live that discourages you from taking alternative transport options?

- If you use a car, what events could you travel to on foot, by bicycle, or on public transport?
- What stops you from car-pooling?

**OBSERVE YOUR PRESENT**

- My primary mode of transport is . . .
- What I like about this way of traveling is . . .
- What I find stressful about this form of travel is . . .
- I am dependent on this way of traveling because . . .

**REFLECT ON YOUR PAST**

- As a child, what I learned about travel and transport was . . .
- I learned to have the relationship I have with Transport by . . .
- The inciting incident I can pinpoint to my current relationship with Transport is . . .
- The way my current relationship with Transport developed over time was . . .

**CONSIDER THE PLANET**

- The impact on nature and the planet from the way I live in my Transport domain is . . .

**CELEBRATE**

- Life-giving skills I have learned and developed in my Transport domain are . . .

If you are ready to continue with the **OREDA** design process for this domain, go to **Envision** on page 158.

## LAND

The Land domain differs from the Nature domain, in that with Land you are in some way tethered to it. Maybe you have a garden, several acres, a plot in a community garden, or a balcony with room for some plant pots. Whatever our ownership relationship is with the land, we need to explore how we can look after it by setting up regenerative systems rather than exploiting it. How can we responsibly and restoratively steward the land in our life?

The Land domain plays a pivotal role in your Homestead realm. Interacting with nature through tending and growing food and other plants gives you a direct way of being grounded in nature's life force and, in turn, regenerating your own. Having a Land domain increases your possibility of designing a regenerative life. By connecting the inputs and outputs from your house and your land, you can start to create integrated, regenerative systems that support life. It's possible to do this even if you live in an apartment. When I lived in an apartment in New York City, I enjoyed growing food and being in nature at a local community garden, where I took my kitchen scraps to contribute to the community compost bin.

Mainstream gardening practices tend to involve ample use of chemical fertilizers and pesticides, which kill the life in the soil. The plants grown are often inedible ornamental flowers or shrubs that might look beautiful but take up space where food could be grown.

If you have access to land, you have a bit of nature with which you can begin to interact and to which you can start to direct beneficial nutrients from your house. Look for opportunities to design your homestead in such a way that the systems you have to meet your needs within your home are integrated with your land systems. You might grow fruit trees on your land, and the gray water from your kitchen sink and washing machine could be redirected to water the trees.

You could even begin to work with your neighbors to create larger-scale microclimates that can work as a response to environmental collapse by restoring habitat that encourages biodiversity—plants and animals to repopulate your bioregion. A healthy, regenerating ecosystem will, in turn, play a role in safe carbon disposal through carbon capture and seques-tration, which will help to mitigate climate change. It's time to take the fences down and look at ways to collaborate. By seeing your land and your neighbors as part of a greater whole, rather than a subdivision, you can collaborate on soil restoration and rainwater harvesting to create a microclimate in ways you couldn't possibly do alone.

What we do today with our land, and especially with how we culti-vate living soil, will be the most important legacy we can leave for future generations.

**OBSERVE YOUR PRESENT**

- When it comes to my Land domain, I . . .
- The life-affirming aspects of my relationship with the Land domain are . . .
- The degenerative aspects of my relationship with the Land domain are . . .

**REFLECT ON YOUR PAST**

- As a child, the Land domain was . . .
- I found positive Land domain role models by . . .

**CONSIDER THE PLANET**

- The impact on nature and the planet from that the way I live in my Land domain is . . .

**CELEBRATE**

- Life-giving skills I have learned and developed in my Land domain are . . .

If you are ready to continue with the **OREDA** design process for this domain, go to **Envision** on page 158.

## AFFECTION REALM

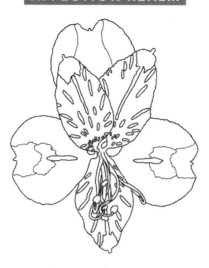

The three Affection domains are about our relationship with people. We relate in different ways and to varying depths with the people in our lives. The challenge with categorizing relationships for the purpose of this Life Design process is that our lives are unique and often don't fit neatly into simple categories. We have relationships with intimate companions, family members, friends, co-workers and colleagues, acquaintances, and people outside our immediate realm—strangers who may become friends or companions. For the purpose of your Life Design in Affection, we will focus on three relationship domains: Family (of origin), Friends, and Intimate Companion.

This introduction to the Affection realm is longer than previous domain introductions because while the domain descriptions focus on the nuances of each of these relationships, some awareness and skills can be ascribed to all three domains, so I will cover them in this introduction.

I called this realm Affection because when these relationships are regenerative, affection lies at the heart of what we seek to give and receive. I'm using Affection as a way of expressing a range of things we are seeking in relationships with others. We want a sense of connection. We want to be affirmed. We want to receive empathy and be understood. When we experience pain, we want to feel that someone understands what we are experiencing. Affection relationships are the source of our sense of belonging and safety, identity, and understanding. In these relationships, we hope to experience empathy and trust.

Regenerative relationships in the Affection realm are the ones in which you predominantly give to the other person, rather than expecting to get or take. When we abide in our sovereignty, we have access to our own power. We don't need to seek validation or depend on anyone else's power to get power. We have more to give because we are naturally connected to our sense of who we are and our life force. If all parties are grounded in their sovereignty, they are more likely to be naturally in giving mode, and with everyone giving, everyone is receiving. We have and create relationships of mutual trust.

When you begin the Life Design process in Affection, I encourage you to start with Family, then Friends, and finally Intimate Companion. This order follows the flow of influence these domains had on the development of your worldviews and values, in the way you relate with others and how you live life. If you feel a strong pull to approach these domains in a different order, follow your intuition.

Working in these domains, you will explore how regenerative and life-affirming your relationships are. In reality, many of our relationships are not as life-affirming as they could be. It's possible that most of us have never deeply felt that trusting, empathetic care and affection that we long for. We were likely not given any guidance in creating regenerative, life-affirming relationships.

Five life-diminishing habits in relationships are: being controlling, making assumptions, gossiping, one-sided sharing of one's problems, and being unable to say no. These habits can be present in all three Affection domains and are worth being aware of as you do your Life Design. In what circumstances do you engage in these habits, or are you on the receiving end?

Relationships become messy when the other person or we ourselves try to control rather than influence each other. In trusting relationships within the Affection realm, we welcome the influence of the other, and vice versa. This influence may occur in things we or others say or do. We are entrusted with the possibility of influence because we are open to that person or they are open to us.

The means of control can occur in different ways: through the mind and our thoughts by saying undermining and unkind things, through the body with physical aggression, or with an expression of emotion that ascribes blame. Relationships in all three domains can be abused in this way, and shift from the gentle and trusting quality of influence to the strong-arming desire to control. Intimate Companion and Family are the two domains in which there's a deeper commitment, one by choice and the other by birth to the people who form the relationship with you, so recognizing where your need for control arises and exploring how you can relate differently with your loved one is essential if you want to become more life-affirming.

Making and holding onto assumptions about another person is a common habit, which keeps us disconnected from one another. Rather than relating to the person, we are relating to the layer of assumptions we've covered them with. Holding onto these assumptions separates us from the person and creates misunderstanding. Developing a practice of noticing when you have an assumption about someone and asking them if it is valid gives them the opportunity to corroborate or burst your assumption. Then you are actually in relationship with them, rather than with your own assumptions.

Gossip and having assumptions about someone are connected. When we gossip, we complain about, criticize or condemn a person's behavior— not to them but to a third party. Often our assumptions are the source of our gossip. Gossip is a degenerate and demoralizing pattern to get into. We often gossip when we feel powerless in our own life. This powerlessness may be linked to the person we are gossiping about. Or maybe the person we gossip with holds some power over us. We may gossip due to unresolved emotional pain from this relationship or a relationship in our past.

Gossip may feel like an innocent activity. You may complain to a friend that your lover didn't do something you assumed they would do. You might criticize small things that your son or daughter does. It's a slippery slope because our judgmental mind will always find something to complain about. At some point, you might have infused your relationship with your lover or friend with so much that is wrong with them that it has become impossible for them to do anything right.

When someone frequently complains about the behavior of a partner, family member, or friend, there may be something genuinely wrong or abusive in the relationship, which the complainer is unable to confront. This is where you need to check your assumptions about someone and find out if something genuinely harmful or life-threatening is occurring.

Have you ever had the experience of being with a friend who overshares and talks at length about their problems? They take up all the time you have together talking about what's wrong with their life, and they do it every time you meet. When you part, you feel drained or have a sense of sticky energy—the person has just unloaded their distress on you without permission, or maybe you have done this to a friend. Turning your friends into substitute therapists is inappropriate. Family members and friends can be empathetic people to share your problems with, but only if you have a mutual agreement that this is part of what you do together.

Being unable to say no to people when they ask us to do things we don't want to do is often referred to as having a "lack of boundaries." This is another way that we lose energy and our sovereignty. We may be afraid of saying no because we're worried the person will withdraw their friendship altogether, or we're concerned we will hurt their feelings. We go along with what they want while feeling uncomfortable or incongruent.

Whichever domain you are working in, you want to be able to connect with others while being rooted in yourself. It's worth learning or refreshing the fundamental skills to help you do this, including communication, empathy, and conflict transformation. Doing your self-care work in the Well-Being domains will also go a long way toward supporting you in bringing a life-affirming approach to relationships.

Communication is a core skill we need for all the Affection domains. Different qualities of communication are used in different situations. We use our communication skills to discuss ideas, make decisions together, or share how we feel about something. The depth of our relationship will influence our communication style, and not necessarily for the better. With friends, we might communicate with a level of informality we wouldn't use with family. Or we might treat family members with a degree of disregard that we'd never bestow upon our friends.

The communication skills we may already have or need to develop are: speaking concisely, listening with our full attention, asking open questions, and at times, reflecting back what we heard by paraphrasing. When there is a high level of trust, established through the recognition of shared values and worldview, the communication can be rapid and fluid, and you may not need to use all of these skills, or you may use them so naturally that you aren't aware of it. If you're curious about the other person, you're probably employing these skills naturally. When a relationship is strained or we are in conflict, and there is a greater need to express our desire for connection, we need to slow down the exchanges. Using these communication skills will help the process.

There are two roles in communication: the person speaking and the person or people listening. When you are the person speaking, practice speaking concisely; that is, express yourself succinctly and get to the point. People listening to you will be able to follow what you're saying easily and understand the point you wish to make. If you talk for too long and add points that are not connected to the one you want to make, you are more likely to confuse and frustrate them or lose their attention. Speaking concisely demonstrates a desire to share the space and time you have together and that you are interested in the other's perspectives, not just your own. Speaking concisely contributes in regenerative ways to the conversation and the relationship by supporting a natural flow of energy through words.

When we are in the listening role, the practice of deep listening can enhance the sense of connection. When we listen deeply, we give the person speaking our full attention. We listen from our heart as well as our mind. We are fully present to what the person is saying. There is no need for us to be thinking about what to say in response. If we are thinking of a response, we aren't really hearing what the person is saying.

Deep listening doesn't necessarily mean we need to make eye contact. It is possible to listen deeply to someone without making eye contact. This approach needs to be understood among the people communicating with one another, though, if it is not the cultural norm.

When the person has made their point, you can reflect back what you've heard them say by paraphrasing and checking if you have understood them correctly. This way they can confirm that what you heard them say is indeed what they said. You can engage your curiosity and use open questions that invite them to expand on what they have been saying. When you use open questions, you can elicit more details, whereas closed questions usually lead to a yes or no answer.

Listening deeply can become hard when someone is talking with emotion about something that perhaps resonates with or triggers your own emotions. If you've done your work in Express and Presence, it will be easier to simply be present as the person speaks.

If you engage these core communication skills, you will naturally begin to build your empathy muscle—your heart—because you will be engaging; that is, listening and reflecting in a way that invokes empathy. These skills also assist in minimizing conflict. Conflict can occur as a result of not understanding the other person's point of view or what they experience. With these skills, you will have the capability to slow down the communication when things get confusing. By paraphrasing, you reflect back what you heard the person say, which can bring clarity into the communication.

I have touched on a few habits and skills that are quick to read about but take practice to learn or unlearn, and embody.

You will recover a great deal of your life force by working through these domains. You will identify what it is you can do more of to nurture these relationships so that they are mutually beneficial. You will uncover relationship patterns that suck the life force out of you and the people you are in a relationship with. If you discover that a relationship with someone in your life lacks mutually beneficial intentions, you can design ways to transform them. If you find imbalances in any of these domains, either through your behavior or that of the other, it doesn't necessarily mean that you need to end the relationship. This can be your opportunity to practice your skills in authentic and honest communication and uncover healthier ways of relating with one another.

The Life Design process is intended to help you identify where your life force is trapped and to take action to recover it. As with all other domains, you will have thought seeds to prompt you into a journaling process. As you journal, you may uncover some deep-seated emotions that are too much for you to work through alone. This is where you can use the Envision and Define process to get yourself into a supportive situation with a therapist or counselor.

## FAMILY

In Family, the invitation is for you to focus on your family of origin, or if you were adopted, both your family of origin and your adopted family. It may be that, as an adult, you chose a surrogate family made up of close friends, or you may have created a family of your own. The focus of our Life Design work, however, is to recover your life force in relation to the family you grew up in.

Our life force is often trapped in the beliefs and stories we hold about our childhood family and the experiences we had with them. The challenge with exploring your family is that it isn't simply about your two-way relationship with your mother or your father or your siblings. You and your family members were and are part of a system in which patterns and dynamics were formed. Unconsciously, you will have adopted a role, the golden child or the black sheep, perhaps. These roles are life-limiting and remain part of you until you uncover and release them.

In the introduction to Affection, I described the fundamental positive attributes of healthy, life-giving relationships. Maybe you were fortunate to grow up in a family in which you were nurtured and supported to be your full self. Or perhaps you have already started the process of exploring and transforming life-limiting themes from your childhood. If neither of these is the case, this is your opportunity to begin examining the relationships you had as a child with your family members and discovering how you can recover your life force. I purposely put Affection after Well-Being and Homestead so that through the work you did in those two areas, you have recovered energy that will help you in your work on relationships.

As you follow this process, you may uncover memories that bring up strong emotions; for example, anger, sadness, fear, or shame. Your work is to be with the emotions, as described in the Express domain. The process will not be constructive or regenerative if you allow yourself to get caught up in blaming people or seeking retribution. This work is about you designing the life you wish to live now. To do this, you need to recover your life force, not continue to tie it up in the past. It may well be that the emotions that come up for you are strong, and there is a tendency to avoid going into the emotions by getting distracted by stories of blame. If this is the case, find someone to support you, ideally a therapist who encourages you to express your emotions and use physical movement, rather than one who has you sit in a chair recounting the story over and over.

Our family is where our beliefs and identity were formed, yet we are so much more than our beliefs and the identity we took on. As children, we naturally have a need to belong, and it is through receiving affection, primarily from our parents, that we gain that sense of connection. We learned through keen observation of adults and older siblings around us that if we behaved in particular ways, we were more likely to get affection.

In most families, even in the most loving ones, the love we receive is conditional. This is the beginning of how we take on our family's worldview, which is consciously or unconsciously held up as the measure of our behavior. If what we do is aligned with our parents' worldview, we are more likely to gain love. If we go against it, we might experience rejection, conflict, and painful feelings. What makes it even more complex is that our mother and our father will each have their own worldviews, the ones they received from their family of origin and life experiences. This means that we often grow up with a mixture of worldviews that we are measured against.

As children, we don't understand that there are different worldviews at play, and as adults, we might not necessarily be conscious of this either. When two different worldviews meet, there's potential for conflict. A conflict might be something as minor as a tension in the air, or someone might withdraw and stop communicating, or it might involve extreme expressions of emotion. You may have experienced this happening with your parents.

If we don't examine our Family domain, we leave our life force trapped in those stories from the past. We continue to lose precious life force through unfinished business with a family member—life force that could help us think and act meaningfully for our collective future.

You might have a strong emotional charge, usually with painful feelings, or spend considerable time going over events that took place in the past. This typically indicates that there's unfinished business with a family member. You can continue to lose energy, even if that family member is dead, by continuously going over something negative they said or did. Regurgitating events that caused you pain is a good indicator that you are hooked by them and are losing energy.

You may have charges from experiences with siblings as well as your parents. Sibling rivalry can arise for all kinds of reasons. The eldest child may feel ousted by the next child who comes along, seeming to take up all of the parents' attention. This older sibling might behave in cruel ways toward or reject their younger brother or sister as a way of dealing with their hurt.

As you grew up, you might have experienced a range of psychological and emotional behavior from family members. This could include a parent or sibling withholding or withdrawing connection, being overly emotional toward you, or being manipulative. If this is the only behavior we experience as children, we accept this as normal. Even in the most loving families, children can experience emotional abuse. Parents don't necessarily intend it; they might just not have the experience or understanding themselves to know how to give authentic affection. Events that happen within the family constellation that can create emotional or psychological trauma include divorce, death, secrets, and affairs.

The process of exploring your Family domain can bring up painful emotions, but it is worth it. What you are looking for is a relationship with each family member in which you can be with them or think about them without feeling energetically pulled by the things they say or do. You want to arrive at a place in your life where your identity is liberated from being defined by or trying to prove yourself to your mother, your father, or a sibling. You want to be liberated from the family dynamics.

- Which family members do you still hold a charge with?
- What stories or beliefs do you have about what you need to do to gain affection?
- Which family member are you still trying to prove yourself to?
- Which family member did you feel alive with?
- Which family member did you have a life-diminishing relationship with?

Use the thought seeds to reflect and journal about each family member with whom you feel a residual charge.

**OBSERVE YOUR PRESENT**

- My relationship with (family member) is . . .
- Life-affirming aspects of my relationship with her/him are . . .
- Life-diminishing aspects of my relationship with her/him are . . .
- What I appreciate about (family member) is . . .

**REFLECT ON YOUR PAST**

- When I was a child, my (family member) was . . .
- My (family member) was a role model for me by . . .
- Things I appreciated about my (family member) were . . .
- What I find challenging in my relationship with my (family member) is . . .

**CONSIDER THE PLANET**

- The impact on nature and the planet from my relationship with (family member) is . . .

**CELEBRATE**

- Life-giving skills I have learned and developed through my relationship with (family member) are . . .

You can either complete the **Observe and Reflect** part of the process for all family members, or go on to **Envision** on page 158 for the one you are focusing on.

Remember: We're not doing this work to find someone to blame; this process is about you recovering your energy from the situation and moving on. Your family is a system. By working on your relationship with one family member, you will bring changes to the whole family system—and if you have a positive intention, these changes are usually for the better.

## FRIENDS

The Friends domain is all about your friendships. Doing Life Design work in your Friends domain will help you get clear on which friendships are mutually life-giving, which ones leave you feeling drained and used, and which ones you contribute to in a life-diminishing way. This is an opportunity for you to be honest with yourself about how you nurture and cherish your friendships and to make changes for the better where needed.

We can fall into friendships, or we can choose them. A friend differs from an acquaintance by the depth of interest, care, concern, and empathy in the relationship, as well as the time we give to it. Friendship usually starts when a bond forms through shared experience or common interest. Friends can come into our lives at different stages. You may have a best friend you met when you were both children or at school. You may have a group of friends from your days at a workplace. Or maybe you make friends in each new environment you enter. Friendships meet our need for belonging and play a role in maintaining or developing our identity. You may have different friends to meet different needs or support different parts of your identity.

Earlier on, I wrote about the positive, regenerative qualities of relationships. In the domain of Friends, the invitation is to root out the friendships in which either you or your friends are playing a life-diminishing role. Then you can envision the friendships you truly want, and design how you can contribute to that happening. With this in mind, I am going to highlight some challenging life-diminishing behaviors in friendships in order to stimulate your thinking. You may think of other behaviors to include.

Friendships can become energy drains when we start to sleepwalk in them. We can take them for granted, expecting our friends to be there for us without putting in the effort to nourish the friendship.

You might have slipped into an exhausting competitive status game, in which you have the habit of always one-upping your friends. You might have developed controlling habits that propel you to always lead and dominate the conversation. Perhaps you don't listen to what your friends are saying because you're only waiting to make your point or share your own even better experience. Maybe you talk incessantly and have no interest in hearing about your friend's experience. Perhaps you are on the receiving end of this behavior, or you both do some or all of it to one another. Neither one of you is giving. Both of you only desire to receive.

You may find that in your relationship with friends, you unconsciously recreate patterns from your childhood. You treat your friends in the way you were treated by your family or by a specific family member. This way of treating your friends is not good for either of you.

It might be that you have had a transformative experience, and you find that you can no longer relate to your friends. It might be something as simple as you finally making and following through with a commitment to look after your health, not drinking alcohol or eating unhealthy food. If part of how you socialized with your friends was drinking and eating out, you have to find new ways to maintain your friendship, without losing your new sense of self-worth.

At a time when we need to be healing our relationship with nature and the planet, living with toxic friendships is a waste of precious energy. We can play a positive role by cleaning them up, not necessarily by abandoning them but rather by inviting our friends into our Life Design process. Together, you can consciously explore the life-diminishing contributions you make to the relationship and identify specific things you could do to make it what you both genuinely want for each other. If you feel something thorny or unpleasant in a relationship with a friend, on some level they will be feeling it too. Part of your process toward sovereignty is to reach out and invite them to join you in figuring out how to cherish your relationship.

What do you love about your friends? (You can get specific about individual friends or a group.)

- In what ways are your friendships regenerative and life-giving?
- How do you contribute to your friendship in life-giving ways?

- In which circumstances, or with whom, do you play status games?
- In what kind of situation do you feel the need to control the conversation?
- Which friends leave you feeling drained?
- What conscious communication skills do you use with your friends?
- What unexplored assumptions do you have about your friends?
- What assumptions do you think they have about you?
- When do you gossip with or about friends or other people?

Using the thought seeds, first establish why friendships are important to you. Then think about specific friendships that leave you feeling drained, and use the thought seeds to explore what it is about these friendships that make them life-diminishing, and in what ways from your perspective do you and your friends contribute to this state.

**OBSERVE YOUR PRESENT**

- My friendships are important to me because . . .
- What I appreciate about (friend's name) is . . .
- My relationship with (friend's name) is . . .
- Life-affirming aspects of my relationship with her/him are . . .
- Life-diminishing aspects of my relationship with her/him are . . .
- What I find challenging in my relationship with (friend's name) is . . .

**REFLECT ON YOUR PAST**

- As a child, my friendships were . . .
- I made friends by . . .
- Friends who were life-affirming role models for me were . . . (name them)
- Specific things I appreciated about (same friend's name) were . . .

**CONSIDER THE PLANET**

- The impact on nature and the planet from the way I live in my Friends domain is . . .

**CELEBRATE**

- Life-giving skills I have learned and developed in my Friends domain are . . .

If you are ready to continue with the **OREDA** design process for this domain, go to **Envision** on page 158.

## INTIMATE COMPANION

The Intimate Companion domain focuses on your relationship with the person with whom you have chosen to share your deeper nature. This is the person with whom you long to be fully known and accepted. In the process of recovering yourself, you may focus your design work on someone you are currently in a relationship with, previous companions, or the companion you long for. The Intimate Companion relationship is one in which you are likely to engage a considerable amount of your life force.

The relationship with an intimate companion is a complex one, in which you and your partner fulfill a number of roles, depending on your circumstances. Your intimacy with the person may have developed by living together, either currently or at some point in your relationship. You may have had children and raised a family with your current Intimate Companion or a previous one. You and your current companion may be child-free. You may be with the same Intimate Companion you married 20–30 years ago, or longer, or you may have had several Intimate Companions throughout your life. Your Intimate Companion may be one person or several.

Being in a relationship with an Intimate Companion is not a prerequisite for a fulfilling life, although the dominant worldview would have us believe otherwise. Many people enjoy a rich solo life, but if you are single and longing for an Intimate Companion, working in this area will help you uncover the needs, wants, and desires you project into this relationship. Working on the domain of Intimate Companion is an opportunity to recover your life force from your longing or from previous relationships. A regenerative Intimate Companion relationship is one in which your partnership supports each of you to thrive. Your energy naturally flows between you. In this relationship, your life force is charged and vital. You are genuinely curious about your intimate companion, and they about you. Your intimate companion is privileged to see you, both when you are in your power and when you're having a bad day. In turn, you have the honor of seeing them in their imperfect humanness as well as their brilliance. When you disagree, you are able to make space and time to share and hear one another's perspectives and constructively arrive at mutual agreement for a way forward. You share power.

Together, you collaborate to create a vibrant yet peaceful and trusting environment in which you can both flourish and unfold the deeper parts of yourself. You can be yourself, and you support one another to evolve emotionally, psychologically, and spiritually. You encourage each other's physical well-being through eating well together, exercising, and making love. If you live together, you share responsibilities, using your natural skills to maintain, operate, and cover the expenses of your shared Homestead. If you are married, you may pay taxes as a couple and have a joint bank account.

You have enough in common to engage with each other's passions, or are willing to compromise to find experiences to share. You have a healthy balance of being and doing things together and having other needs met through friendships. You socialize together and are comfortable when one of you needs to have solitude.

The challenges in an Intimate Companion relationship are many, varied, and probably inevitable at some point in the relationship unless we are suppressing something or are enlightened. The good news is that as long as the challenges aren't life-threatening or psychologically damaging, they are gifts that give us the potential to uncover more about ourselves and grow.

In addition to the five life-diminishing habits I mentioned in the Affection introduction, I'll highlight four of the challenges that might arise in the Intimate Companion domain. As you explore this domain more fully through the thought seeds, you might uncover others.

## Romantic Love

If you start off trying to create a lasting relationship with romantic love as the foundation, you are in for a big surprise. A relationship is not a fairy tale, so don't expect your prince or princess to show up some day. Romantic love is the version of a relationship that is perpetuated by marketing departments, encouraging us to buy and consume their products and services:

*diamonds, chocolates, clothes—if you don't get these things for me, you don't love me.* As if these items were a genuine statement of love and affection. Romance is only part of the relationship, and if you want it, you need to make sure that your partner enjoys it as much as you do.

## Allowing the Relationship to Consume You

Being in an intimate relationship requires an awareness that while you are involved in co-creating the relationship, there is still space for you to be you. It can be all too easy for both of you to draw together in a middle ground, or one of you is pulled all the way into the pocket of your partner, losing your sense of self, your sovereignty. If you are always doing what your partner wants to do, you may have lost sight of who you are and what *you* are interested in.

## Trying to Fix Your Partner

The beautiful thing about being human is that we all come with our imperfections. Looking for the perfect person, or trying to fix the one you're with, is a pointless pursuit. If you are perpetually trying to fix your partner because they don't measure up to your ideal, you will erode any trusting foundation you have. Many of the ideal partner concepts are created and perpetuated by corporate marketing departments and Hollywood scriptwriters.

## Covering Up the Real Issues with Superficial Responses

At some point in a relationship, you will encounter real problems that challenge your relationship. The challenges might start with small yet accumulating behaviors like always coming home late or one of you, or both, losing yourself in the smartphone while with family. They could escalate to one of you having an affair, assuming your relationship is a monogamous one; one of you being constantly verbally abusive or, at times, even physically abusive; or one of you continually undermining the other, blaming your partner for your own emotions, being jealous, or being deceitful.

Covering up these issues with superficial responses happens when there's potential for painful emotions to show up and you don't feel you have the ability to cope with them. One or both of you don't want to feel that pain. There's a reason your partner had an affair—perhaps it's because they don't feel heard or connected to you. There's a reason they always come home hours later than when they say they will. There's a reason why they lose themselves on their smartphone when they're with you and the kids.

Finding a way to connect and explore what's being covered up is a potential step toward strengthening the relationship for the better.

- In what way is your relationship enriching and life-affirming?
- How do you express your affection in your relationship?
- In what ways do you take your Intimate Companion for granted?
- What are the common interests that keep you connected?
- What are the unique, quirky things you love about your Intimate Companion?
- What are the unresolvable relationship patterns you can live with?
- In what ways do you feel limited by your relationship?
- In what ways are you un-healthfully dependent?

If you live with your Intimate Companion:

- How do you share the operating and maintenance activities of your Homestead?
- What financial and practical responsibilities do you share?

If you raised a family together:

- How do you share the responsibility of connecting with your child/children?

**OBSERVE YOUR PRESENT**
- The life-affirming things in my relationship are . . .
- Life-affirming contributions I bring to the relationship are . . .
- Life-affirming contributions my partner brings are . . .
- The life-diminishing things in my relationship are . . .
- Life-diminishing contributions I bring to the relationship are . . .
- Life-diminishing contributions my partner brings are . . .
- The ways I express my affection are . . .
- The things I take for granted in my relationship are . . .
- I appreciate my partner for . . .
- The small daily ways I appreciate my partner are . . .
- The things I appreciate that we create together are . . .
- What makes me want to work things out is . . .

**REFLECT ON YOUR PAST**

- What I could learn from past relationships is . . .

**CONSIDER THE PLANET**

- The impact on nature and the planet from the way I live in my Intimate Companion domain is . . .

**CELEBRATE**

- Life-giving skills I have learned and developed in my Intimate Companion domain are . . .

If you are ready to continue with the **OREDA** design process for this domain, go to **Envision** on page 158.

## EXCHANGE REALM

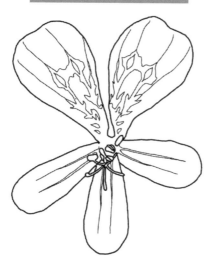

The realm of Exchange contains three domains: Livelihood, Money, and Community. These domains invite us to explore how we exchange our life force by the way we generate an income through work, what we do with the money we earn, and how we can expand and enrich its potential through community. Delving into these domains will help you uncover your beliefs about making a living, money in general, and working in community. You will begin to see how you can design these domains so that they contribute to the planet in a life-giving way.

Most of us live with unexamined beliefs about how we generate our income and what we do with money. We also overlook the possibilities that could emerge if we were willing to share and cooperate with the people who live in the same place as we do. Income generation through livelihood occurs when we use our experience, knowledge, and time and trade it for money. When we buy things, we take that experience, knowledge, and time—now in the form of money—and trade it for something else: we either invest it, so it increases, or we spend it, so it decreases. When we start to view the people who live in our neighborhood as more than just neighbors and begin to cooperate and share, we have the potential for a vastly enriched life that goes well beyond making and spending money. Through local community initiatives we will begin the process of recovering the authenticity of our culture, which grows from a sense of belonging and of place and which can't be imported from a factory on the other side of the planet.

At this time, most people on the planet are involved in ways of earning a living that disregard our collective need to ensure that Earth's life-support systems thrive. The destruction of the planet by humans has not happened out of malice. When the current economic system was established, very recently in terms of human history, the economic thinkers of that time did not have a worldview that included an awareness of the finite nature of the planet. They were oblivious of the time needed for natural systems to regenerate and function. We do have that understanding now. Still, the human-designed systems set up to meet our needs are so deeply entrenched that it is hard to make the urgent and lasting course correction needed at this point in time.

Life Design in this realm is vital. What we do to earn money, and how we spend or invest it, has a significant impact on what is happening to the planet. At the moment, most of us are preoccupied with thoughts somewhere along the spectrum from not having enough money to wondering how we can make more. We overlook how money flows through our lives, and our choices about how to accumulate or use it contribute to the damage that is occurring. By shifting our perspective and uncoupling ourselves from the belief system of the economic worldview, we can have a positive impact; we can become a beneficial part of the system.

I believe that our future will come through working in community. There is so much work to do in response to what's occurring on the planet. Much of it is not valued by the private sector because it doesn't make a profit, but it is still essential for us to have a livable planet. This is where community comes in, as we create community gardens and woodlands, retrieve our local cultures through music and dance, rekindle our relationship with nature, find new ways to look after the young and old people who live near us, and set up collective action for food sovereignty, local energy systems, and community investment projects.

I suggest you work on the domains in the order they are presented in this realm. Livelihood comes first, as this is how most of us earn money. We need to have money before we can do something with it, so the Money domain comes second. Community expands this realm outward beyond your self, your homestead, your affection relationships, and the limits of money, into a place where I believe the potential for a vibrant, thriving future exists.

## LIVELIHOOD

The Livelihood domain is about the way you gain money through work. Redesigning this part of our life has the potential to make a significant intervention in the life-destroying trajectory we're currently on. By working in this domain, we can start to design a pathway to a regenerative livelihood, one that supports the ability of Earth's systems to thrive. The more of us who redirect our life force toward regenerative living and leading, the more significant the beneficial impact will be.

influence change
social enterprise
equal opportunities
regenerative *work you love*
equal pay
# livelihood
*work-life balance* social good
eight capitals ethical business
*empowered workplace*
universal basic income
holistic management
triple bottomline

We need a massive and rapid shift away from degenerative business models, workplace practices, and means of production toward regenerative ones. The way in which products and services are brought to market needs to be reevaluated and redesigned to acknowledge that we live on a finite planet, with limited resources and places to discard our waste. In fact, we need to reevaluate how we meet our needs as a collective. There has to be a way in which we can achieve our Well-Being needs (life-giving food, clean drinking water, climate-appropriate homes, clothing, and transport) without continuing to trash nature's life-support systems.

The challenge for most of us who have to engage with livelihood activities is that the available work is comprised of interwoven and interdependent degenerative systems. The pressure to earn money to live, gain a pension, pay taxes, and pay off debt means that most of us don't have the luxury to be selective about the work we do. The fact is that we also don't have the luxury to continue supporting this unconscious way of doing things and ignoring the alarms being sounded through ceaseless large-scale natural events catalyzed by rising sea levels. You just have to cast your eye over the last few months of global news to read about devastating floods, droughts, forest fires, desertification, earthquakes, hurricanes, and cyclones, which are making life on every continent untenable.

We need the power to bring about changes in the workplace. In our Well-Being domains, we can control how we meet our needs; in the workplace, it's harder to have control. If we own the company, have shares in it, or are in a leadership role, we do have varying degrees of control. With that power, we need to find the courage to make changes to the business model and bring everyone along with us.

If you have your own company, you can rise to the challenge of finding ways to stay in business, pay your employees, and transition to regenerative business practices. If you are a shareholder, you can put pressure on the company to make changes, although you have to be willing to make less of a return on your investment during the transition period and over the long term. If you are in a leadership role, you can start taking the initiative to find feasible ways for your department, or the aspects of the company you are responsible for, to transition and bring your proposals to the company directors and shareholders.

As company employees, we have less control but we may have influence. This comes from our role in the company and our social, intellectual, and experiential capital. Socially, we may have the respect of our employers and/ or our colleagues. We may have experience and knowledge related to the company's business that could help with the design of a regenerative business model. We can use our influence to make a case for the company to move to an immediate transition.

What we can also do is create a degree of flexibility in our own lives by calculating how much we really need to earn to live our life, meet our financial responsibilities, and care for our family. Taking the time to learn how much you really need to earn will help you see if you can afford to look for a different job, one that is part of a regenerative business model.

- What does your workplace do to generate money?
- What are the regenerative practices in your workplace?
- What are the degenerative, destructive practices in your workplace?
- What action could you take to steer the company toward a regenerative design?

- What workplace skills do you have that you could use in a company that does have a regenerative, life-giving production system?
- In what ways do you feel you have a choice about the work you do?
- In what ways do you feel you have no choice about the work you do for a living?
- What were you taught as a child about work and making a living?

**OBSERVE YOUR PRESENT**

- The work I do to make a living is . . .
- The transferable skills I have are . . .
- The ways my work contributes to planetary regeneration is . . .
- The ways my work contributes to planetary degeneration is . . .

**REFLECT ON YOUR PAST**

- As a child, I learned that work was . . .
- From the adults in my life I learned that work was . . .

**CONSIDER THE PLANET**

- The impact on nature and the planet from the way I live in my Livelihood domain is . . .

**CELEBRATE**

- Life-giving skills I have learned and developed in my Livelihood domain are . . .

If you are ready to continue with the **OREDA** design process for this domain, go to **Envision** on page 158.

## MONEY

In the Money domain, the focus is on our relationship with money and how we can work with it to contribute to a regenerative future both in our life and for the planet.

local banks

*slow money* possibility

**community investment**

local currencies     slow return

# money

ethical investment  asset

collaborative consumption

**debt creates money**

**citizen's income**

**credit union**

This is an opportunity to examine our money-related beliefs and behaviors, weed out what's not working for the planet or for us, and bring in beneficial activities. Maybe you share your Money domain with a companion, and because of this, you make joint decisions. Maybe you have very little sovereignty in this domain because your companion earns the money and decides how best to make it work for the family.

Money is a complex subject, with many threads. Along with reflecting on our personal beliefs and behaviors about money, other things worth exploring are how it's made, how it circulates, and how most of it ends up in the hands of a few people. In this context, I'll stick with how we use it in our personal lives, although I will make some statements that might encourage you to look into the subject of money more deeply.

There's an expression: "Money makes the world go round." The way money is used in the current economic system, it may appear to make the world go round but if you look more deeply, you will see that it is making a few people extraordinarily rich, while keeping half the world's population in poverty. The way those people get rich is through business practices that encourage and contribute to the trashing of the planet and people's lives.

Another expression is: "You can't take it with you when you die." Why then do people need to have millions of dollars, amounts far exceeding what is necessary to live a good life, even in retirement? We are encouraged to get upset when politicians suggest that perhaps, through a tiny amount of taxation, the super-wealthy and corporations could put their money to good use helping those who are struggling to get by.

It is astounding that for something we use daily, we were not taught in school how to work with money in a useful, constructive, and life-benefiting way. The only thing we get is advertising, encouraging us to part with our money in exchange for temporary quick fixes that in the long run don't make any real improvements in our life.

Most of us need money to have a home, eat food, clothe ourselves, and travel to and from work or for other purposes. That's it—quite straightforward and pragmatic; yet many people grow up with money beliefs that are tied to their sense of self-worth, so money can become problematic.

Beliefs about money may include "I'm not good enough to have it." If we have money, we may worry that we will never have enough, so we live a frugal life. Some of us may believe that money grows on trees, so we live beyond our means, never save, and are on a constant financial collision course. We think other people will value us for our financial wealth, so we spend money on clothing, a large house, and furniture to show off to people and gain their admiration. Some of us may have grown up with the idea that we don't need to earn money directly; we just marry someone else who makes it.

There are four ways you can gain money: earning it, inheriting it, borrowing it, and winning it. There are four activities you can do with money: spending it, saving it, investing it, and gifting it. Money earned through livelihood comes into our lives through the equation:

**Context + time + energy + knowledge + experience = money**

When we spend money, we exchange it for material items that in most cases depreciate in value over time. When we save it, we put it into a savings account, where it increases slowly in value through interest. When we invest it, we buy items that increase in value as long as they are desirable—real estate, stocks, or gold, for example. We could also invest in our education and professional development.

When we gift it, we can give it to charitable organizations doing work we would like to support. We have needs and wants. A *need* is something that is essential for living; for example, fresh drinking water, food, and shelter. A *want* is something you don't really need, but you think it will somehow improve your quality of life; in this category are luxury items, which are nonessential items that are expensive or hard to get but which you think will make your life more enjoyable. With a worldview that encourages us to consume, we buy more than we need. We're also encouraged to spend money on cheap items and bargains, which are often poorly made or of inferior quality. Poor-quality items break or deteriorate quickly, so we throw them out and put the burden on nature, which has to handle our waste, either because we bury it in the ground, contaminating the soil and groundwater, or we incinerate it and pollute the air.

When we live beyond our means and buy things we don't really need or infrequently use, we bring stress into our lives by having yet another thing we need to deal with. In the end, it's mostly corporations and their shareholders that benefit from the sale of these items that clog up our lives.

Here is a sweeping generalization, one that comes from personal observation of my own habits and that of others: we women do like to surround ourselves with things; that goes for me, too, and I'm not a big shopper. Compared with other women, I have a small wardrobe that includes two purses and eight pairs of shoes, all for different purposes. Compared with my companion, I have a lot of stuff. I know some men do too while some women are minimalist connoisseurs, but on the whole I think that women like to have things. We're like birds feathering the nest, making it cozy and inviting by filling it with things that express our interests and identity. Women have been targeted by marketing departments for generations to spend money on stuff for our beauty, for our appearance, for the home.

Two actions that will improve your relationship with money are to create a monthly budget and to track your spending. The monthly budget is based on your income and living expenses. With this tool, you can see how much you need to earn, and therefore how much you need to work. When you track your spending, you will see how much you spend and what you buy. Doing this you can see where you fritter away your money on nonessential items. Together, these two processes will give you a real picture of your Money domain.

If you have investments, you could calculate the money you will have to live on by the time you reach the age you'd like to retire, and figure out if you still need to work, save, and invest. You might find you are in the fortunate position of having invested at a young age and that you will have more than enough to live comfortably at the age you want to retire. If you have that level of future abundance, you could explore ethical investing. Most wealth-creating investments are made in companies that create life-diminishing and planet-destroying products or services, like oil, tobacco, weapons, or private prisons. If we're really going to play a role in a thriving future, our investments need to align with that vision.

- What beliefs do you have about money that limit your life force?
- What do you do with money that honors your energy?
- How do you use your money to contribute to a thriving future?
- What choices do you make when you spend money?
- What types of businesses do you support when you shop for things?
- What kinds of companies do you support with your investments?
- When you spend money what is your priority?
- What do you spend money on that is nonessential and puts you in a place of living beyond your means?

If you are in an Intimate Companion relationship:

- Do you share the financial responsibilities?
- Who does the investing?
- Do you jointly invest, or does your partner make those decisions?

**OBSERVE YOUR PRESENT**

- The life-affirming beliefs I have about money are . . .
- The life-diminishing beliefs I have about money are . . .
- I use money in regenerative ways by . . .
- I use money in degenerative ways by . . .

**REFLECT ON YOUR PAST**

- As a child, I learned that money was . . .
- The behaviors I learned from my parents about money were . . .

**CONSIDER THE PLANET**

- The impact on nature and the planet from the way I live in my Money domain is . . .

**CELEBRATE**

- Life-giving skills I have learned and developed in my Money domain are . . .

If you are ready to continue with the **OREDA** design process for this domain, go to **Envision** on page 158.

## COMMUNITY

In the Community domain, you have an opportunity to look at ways you can extend your beneficial impact by working with people beyond your Family and Friends domains to take collaborative action.

Communities come into existence when people with a common interest get together. They may be place-based, online, or a combination of the two. For example, you might be involved in a school community because your children attend the school. You meet with the members of that community—the teachers, parents, other students, and administrators—primarily face to face. Or you might be involved in an online gaming community. You've never met any of the people face to face, yet you regularly play games and discuss game strategy with them on the forums. In these and other scenarios, you may use both place-based and online strategies. In the community where I live, for example, I meet with people face to face and also use online platforms for communicating with them.

For the purposes of the Life Design Community domain, we want to create or join communities of interest and place that have a focus on ways to meet our basic needs and wants while nature's life-support systems can still function, regenerate, and flourish.

In our place-based communities we have the opportunity to create a regenerative culture, one that is of the place and informed by the natural world around us. Storytelling, songs, and dances that are informed by our surrounding natural environment can all play a part in enriching our local community and reminding us of what sustains us, what truly matters. Individually, our power over how we meet our needs or bring about change in our communities is limited, but by joining with other people, our potential to be a force for positive change increases exponentially. Working with people can happen by degrees. If you and thousands of other women follow through with your Life Design process and implement something from it, you will have a collective impact without ever having met one another.

Signing an online petition or contributing money to a crowdfunding campaign is another way to have a collective impact without engaging directly with other people. The online platform provides the means for engagement.

The crises we all face are calling us to work together, as working alone, we just won't have a significant impact. We are being asked to connect and learn how to communicate and collaborate with people who may want to contribute to a future for humanity but have a worldview that's different from ours. Through these connections, we have the opportunity to discover more about the world and ourselves.

With people who live in our local community, we can work together to reduce the amount of stuff and energy we consume; for example, by sharing tools, cars, bulk food purchases, and even setting up local renewable energy generation.

Working with other people can be difficult. We may be used to being in control, or people we work with want to be in control. We may think we have the best idea or the best way to do something, and someone else thinks they have the answer.

Even if you do have a good idea for a way forward, if other people don't join you there won't be a collective impact. It will be just you, with other people on the sidelines watching you do it, because they haven't bought into the idea or there wasn't room for them to contribute their own ideas.

When we work in community, tapping into good communication skills is essential. Creating agreements about how to work together is also a great way to begin. In the workplace, those parameters are often done for us, and we learn about them through an induction or the employee handbook. When we work in community, if we aren't explicit in our agreements, we are functioning with assumptions, and at some point these will be tested.

It is a far better use of our energy to take the time to make living agreements. Living agreements are not written in stone and can be changed at any time so that they evolve. Having agreements means that people really know what they're saying yes to, and you are collectively creating an effective and safe collaboration space. It may feel like taking the time to put agreements in place is a digression from getting on with doing the work, but it's well worth it.

An illuminating, often referenced model for group development, proposed by Bruce Tuckman in the 1960s, maps a group's formation through the following stages: Forming, Storming, Norming, and Performing. I use this model in community settings to give people an insight into the underlying process that may be occurring in the group. It doesn't always play out in this way, but it can be useful to have an awareness that it might.

The Forming stage is when the individual members become part of the team or group. They are still polite in their interactions with one another, and they are focused on the task at hand. The Storming stage is when the team members begin to voice their opinion about the work at hand and tensions begin to emerge—the social mask of politeness falls away, giving rise to disagreements. This is a crucial stage of the group development process. If the group is able to navigate the conflicts that arise through skillful and honest communication, and hold onto the reason why they came together in the first place, they will move into the Norming stage, in which they begin to trust each other. During the Norming stage, the group really becomes a group, and its members move into the stride of Performing: working well together.

Doing things in community requires organization. Getting organized can appear to detract from actually getting on with the activities that bring about the change. Being organized as a group demonstrates concern for people's time and energy. Without organization and a strategy, you end up with meetings where those attending get frustrated because there isn't a clear sense that their participation is moving toward action.

There's a tendency in community projects to try to include everyone in every decision. This happens because people who want to create community believe that this is the way to share power. Through observation of community processes I've seen that including everyone in everything is a way for the group to quickly become ineffective and powerless. At times, it can be challenging to entrust people to make decisions on our behalf, but if we live in a democracy, we do place our trust in our elected representatives, so we need to find ways to do the same in our community projects.

There are organizational structures that make it possible to distribute decision-making power within the group and ways of making decisions that involve the process of consent. Sociocracy, for example, is an organizational system that I've been working with, and that's been adopted by many communities and groups in recent years, due to its method of distributing power and built-in feedback systems.

- In what ways do you already do things in community?
- What things could you do in community that would have a beneficial impact on the planet?
- What stops you from working with others outside the workplace?
- What do you learn about yourself when working with others?

**OBSERVE YOUR PRESENT**

- My current experience of community is . . .
- Experiences I find rewarding when working in community are . . .
- What I find challenging about working in community is . . .

**REFLECT ON YOUR PAST**

- As a child, my experience of community was . . .
- I was taught that people I didn't know were . . .

**CONSIDER THE PLANET**

- The impact on nature and the planet from the way I live in my Community domain is . . .

**CELEBRATE**

- Life-giving skills I have learned and developed in my Community domain are . . .

If you are ready to continue with the **OREDA** design process for this domain, go to **Envision** on page 158.

# CHAPTER 9

# Envision

Once you've completed Observe and Reflect, through journaling on your present and past relationship with a domain, the third step in the design process is to Envision your future.

You are envisioning your Sovereign Self, the you that has recovered her life force and power and is living an enriched life that serves both your authentic self and the planet. Who are you one year or five years from now? What are you feeling? What are you doing?

Choose how far into your future you want to envision yourself—one year, five years, or another time frame that makes sense to you. For some domains, you might explore both a short and a more extended period, and uncover different information for each of them. For example, for your Home domain, using two time frames, in one year you might envision that you have your home organized in a way that works for you, and in five years you might be living in an entirely new setting.

Use the following thought seeds, and allow your responses to flow without any self-censorship. Write your observations and discoveries in your journal. You may have other thought seeds you'd like to use.

For the purpose of the Envision process, use the ones provided before adding new ones.

When I envision my life-affirmed self one year (five years) from now:

- I am . . . (describe the qualities your Sovereign Self has in relation to this domain)
- I feel . . . (describe the feelings your Sovereign Self has in relation to this domain)
- I have . . . (describe what your Sovereign Self has in relation to this domain)
- I do . . . (describe what your Sovereign Self is doing in relation to this domain)

- The environment in which this happens is . . . (describe where your Sovereign Self is in relation to this domain)
- My relationship with nature supports me in this domain by . . . (describe how your Sovereign Self works with nature in a way that supports her to live most fully in this domain)

Once you have completed the thought seeds, read through what you've written, and add anything more that comes up.

At the end of the book, I've included exercises in Resources that will allow you to gather further insights and energy from the wisdom of your body, nature, and death in your Observation, Reflection, and Envision processes.

You have now completed the **ORE** part of **OREDA**. You have observed your current life and reflected on your past, and you have envisioned your Sovereign Self in a specific domain. The next step is to take this raw and rich material and use it to inform what you Define as action for change.

# CHAPTER 10

# Define

In Define, you generate ideas for the acts of change your current self can say yes to and embark on in order to become the Sovereign Self you envision. Using the thought seeds provided to develop your idea and describe the change, transition, or nudge you'd like to bring about, you will move through the following steps:

- Gather
- Sort
- Select
- Define

Begin the process with **Gather** by generating as many ideas for actions as you can come up with, then in **Sort** you sort through the ideas, and in **Select**, choose one to focus your energy and creativity on in **Define**.

Yes, narrowing things down is necessary; you'll be doing this frequently as you move through this process. It could be that when you were working in a domain, you got a clear and strong sense of an action you want to take. If that's the case, honor your intuition, and stick with it. You can skip the first three steps and turn to Define on page 163 to develop the details of the actions you are going to take.

## Gather

Gather is where you collect all the ideas for changes you could make in the domain you are working with in one place. The actions might involve changing something physically in yourself or your environment, or it might be changing the way you relate with people or situations. Whatever comes up, write it down. Give yourself a time frame for this, say 5–10 minutes. Rapidly list every idea that comes up, and let your ideas flow. There are no crazy ideas; everything is of value—no censorship here. At the end of this time, stop and read through the ideas you've generated, and write down any additional ones that pop up.

Start the Gather process on a new page in your journal, leaving about a quarter of an inch on the left side for numbering the actions in the next step, and use the following thought seed to begin this process of generating ideas:

- Actions I could take, or changes I could make, that will move me toward my Sovereign Self in relation to this domain are . . .

When the flow of ideas stops, or the time is up, that's the end of your gathering process.

## Sort

Next comes the sorting process. Without getting caught up in trying to get this absolutely right, number the actions in order of priority—the criteria being appropriate changes that move you toward your Sovereign Self and the support of nature's regeneration. Use your intuition or gut feeling for this. Your No. 1 is the action that makes you catch your breath—in excitement, intrigue, enthusiasm; not the easy one you could just do, but the one that sparks your imagination and inspires you.

It could be that an item is actually a smaller step of another action. For example, in my Nature domain, one of the actions I wrote down that allows me to move toward my Sovereign Self was to design a tasting menu and then grow the food for it in my garden, so I could make all these delicious morsels and share them with visitors. This item took my breath away, so I made it No. 1. Other items on the list turned out to be steps within this act, including making a list of things to grow and engaging with the cycle of planting, tending, harvesting, processing, and eating.

You might also find that there are actions that carry different weight. One might involve a longer or deeper commitment, while another might be something you could do right away. An easy item on my list was to sit and observe nature for 10 minutes a day, while another was to bring animals into my life—sheep, perhaps; two very different propositions that would have radically different impacts in my life, and one that is much easier for me to implement immediately.

As you go through the process, you may find that there are items you don't want to number. The idea was good when you came up with it, but now after a few minutes it doesn't seem relevant or engaging. Then just skip it. This part of the process is to clarify what you really want to take action on. When there are no restrictions, we can come up with all kinds of ideas, but when it comes to honing in on what we really want to bring to life and what it would take to realize the ideas we have, then we start to make choices. The mind is a trickster at times, enticing us into all kinds of unnecessary wanting.

Once you've numbered all the actions you want to include, move on to Select.

## Select

If you try to implement too many actions at once, you will become overwhelmed. To ensure that doesn't happen in this step, you will work with the item you identified as No. 1. This is the first action in this domain that you will explore more deeply. Use the following thought seeds to go deeper into your Select process:

- If I could choose only one specific action to ignite, it would be . . .
- I feel resonance and aliveness when I sense into this action because . . .
- Choosing this specific action is thrilling because . . .
- In making this change, I will benefit by . . .
- This life change supports my sovereign values by . . .
- This life change supports my values for caring for the planet by . . .
- Focusing on this life change is worth the time, energy, and money required to reach it because . . .

At the end of this process you will have a stronger sense of this being the action you are going to commit to, or not. If it still feels like it's the one, move on to the next step. Or return to your list in Sort if you realized, through deeper exploration, that it's not the action for you at this time.

If you have difficulty knowing what action to take, you could use the following thought seeds to do a self-survey in your journal. There may be things you didn't go into during your past and present reflections that you need to bring to the surface.

- The obstacles that stand between me and my Sovereign Self in this domain are . . . *(list what you sense are obstacles)*
- I can overcome these obstacles by . . .

## Define

The final step is to Define the actions it will take for you to realize your Sovereign Self in this domain. In your journal, use the thought seeds in the box below to list the specific actions you will take to achieve this life shift. Give each step a number. To help you think through some key actions to get you going, review how you Envision yourself with this one specific experience in your life and then think of the key actions you need to take to get there.

> - The specific action steps I can take to make this change in this domain are . . . (make a list of action steps; again let the ideas flow)
> - Information I need to gather to support my success in making this change is . . .
> - The preparations I need to make that will support me in making this change are . . .
> - When I take action to make these changes in my life, the people I need to consider are . . .
> - What I can do tomorrow is . . .
> - What I can do this month is . . .
> - What I can do this year is . . .

## Methods for Staying on Track

Things you can do to help you stay on track in carrying out your action include the following:

### Affirmation

Affirmations are positive statements you can use to raise your confidence. You can use them when you're doing your activity. For example, you might have the affirmation "I am strong" when you're doing physical exercises.

You may immediately have a sense of what affirmation you want to use. If not, skim through what you've written in the Observe, Reflect, and Envision sections of this domain for clues on which affirmation could assist you as you keep your commitment to these changes.

Affirmations are not for everyone. I use them for some parts of my life, particularly when I'm doing something that involves physical exertion or brings up fear. When I started swimming again, two experiences during which I almost drowned came up for me, so even though I was just in the local pool, I experienced a strong fear of drowning when I was in the deep end. To help me move through the fear I used the affirmation *I am a silver bullet* and then I focused on the underwater light on the wall at the other end of the pool. Using this affirmation, I was able to keep moving through the water without panicking.

- An affirmation I can use to support me as I transition to even more life-affirming ways is . . .

### Imagery

Visualizing yourself as your Sovereign Self reinforces your belief and keeps you excited. As well as visualizing yourself, you can also draw or make collages that depict you as your Sovereign Self.

- The imagery I can use to support me to be sovereign in this domain is . . .
- I will use these images when I am . . .

### Map for Action

Now that you've defined what actions you're going to take toward change, the next step is to schedule when you will act on them. Transformation happens when you make space and time for it.

At this point in the process, you will either have an action plan for each of the 21 domains, or you will have action plans for the domains you honed in on as a result of doing the Spider Web assessment.

Now you can decide when, during the next 12 months, you will begin each change process. This isn't an exercise written in stone. In my journal, I have one page for my mapped actions, and I use the opposite page to map what actually happened. This way I learn how much I'm able to stay on track and how often emergent events come up that I have to or want to respond to.

Deepening your sense of sovereignty in all of your domains at the same time might be too much change for you to handle. If you try it, you might very well be overwhelmed and any actions you implement might unravel. Thinking well about what change you're going to bring into your life and when, in relation to what you've already got going on, will increase the likelihood of your success.

If you've designed a change process to stop eating meat for two months, and you start that change just before a holiday season when your family traditionally eats meat, you're going to have an additional challenge or two. You would either have to restrain yourself or give yourself more work by having to make different meals for others while you experiment with new vegetarian recipes. A better approach is to schedule that change for when you have time to really explore this new direction without conflicting events or requirements.

While making changes in more than one domain at a time may be too much, you could consider working on a Well-Being change while at the same time working on a change in one of the other domains. You could take on your Well-Being Embody action plan to be able to run five kilometers by the end of 60 days and at the same time initiate your Stuff action plan for getting rid of your clutter.

As you worked through Observe, Reflect, and Envision and the steps in Define, it may have become clear to you which changes you want to work on first. If not, look through your journal at the action plans you've designed. This selection process is about trusting your gut, your intuition. What feels right in relation to ongoing commitments you already have? There's part of you that already knows what to start with. Trust what comes, and don't second-guess yourself. If you find yourself standing in a cluttered room with piles of disorganized stuff, and your vision of the home of your Sovereign Self is one where everything has a place, then perhaps that's the place to start.

Scheduling your actions is simple. Take a page in your journal or a separate piece of paper that you can pin up on your notice board, and draw a 12-box grid on it: three across and four down. Make sure that each box is large enough for you to write the title or code related to your action in it. These boxes represent 12 months, and the four rows are the four quarters of the year. Write the initial of each month in the box. For example, if you are starting this process at the beginning of the year, you will begin with J for January.

Now fill the boxes with the actions you want to take, factoring in the 60 days—two months—it takes for a new habit to take root and feel embodied. As you map for action, consider designing in some space for not doing anything; in fact, this could be one of your actions: to learn the practice of doing nothing. That may seem counterintuitive for a Life Design approach to change, but designing downtime, unplanned time, into your life is a powerful and transformative act.

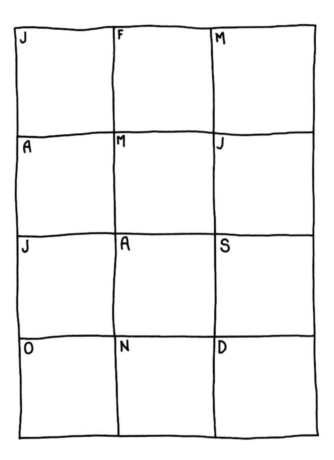

### Commitment

Once you've mapped out the next 12 months, commitment is the next step. This means that you embrace the attitude of just beginning it. Remember that beginning doesn't necessarily mean you are rushing around making things happen. Beginning might take place on your inner plane, where you inwardly dedicate your attention and intention toward taking action.

A NOTE ABOUT ACTION: I want to be clear about what I mean by action in the context of Life Design. Your change may be that you need to make more time for doing nothing. Believe it or not, making that possible involves taking action. Doing nothing involves the action of doing nothing, and at times in life is essential.

## Track

Tracking your actions can help you stay aware of the changes you are making. A tracking system is easy to set up. This could be a simple list of the changes you are going to make, with the days of the month across the top of the page.

Some of your action plans might involve daily activities, others weekly. I use a page in my A5 journal for tracking. You could use the badge icon app on your iPhone, or 30 pebbles, one for each day of the month, to track your accomplished activity. The accumulation of marks on the pages, icon badges in the app, or moved pebbles becomes a way of celebrating your incremental success.

The key to tracking your actions is to keep the system you use simple to set up, so you will actually use it. You can even track existing habits that you would like to stop. Tracking how many days you drink coffee in relation to your not being able to sleep can be a great reality check. I thought that I didn't consume that much sugar because I didn't add it to food. When I started to track it, I found that I was eating it almost daily. It was in pre-prepared food, so I wasn't aware of how much I was actually eating. That motivated me to design a change to cut down on sugar-filled snacks.

## Keeping the Vision Alive

Now that you have a Sovereign Self Life Design map to keep you on track, put it in a place where you can refer to it. You also have your affirmations, as well as tools to use should limiting beliefs and patterns appear. I should write *when* they appear, as they will. Don't leave your Life Design journal lying around to gather dust or stashed in a cupboard. Take it with you, and use it.

You've taken the time to observe your life, both how you live it now and how you've lived it in the past. You've envisioned your Sovereign Self, defined the changes you want to make, and mapped them for action. Now it's time to act. Implementing the Act part of the Life Design process has a certain rhythm; sometimes you will be doing, other times you will be being. How you create change in your life will impact it for the duration of its existence. The old way of doing things tended to involve forcing things to happen. Another habit to let go of is to talk about doing something until all the zest has gone out of it. The Act part of Life Design involves being, listening, and acting as a response to prompts that emerge in your life.

By designing even one life change, you have invited life to dance with you, to respond to you, and support you. It will continue to do so, as long as you show up.

It can be easy as well as painful to get stuck in the Observe, Reflect, Envision, or Define steps of Life Design. The real action—including the magic—happens when you start to implement change—to Act. By bringing it to life you become your Sovereign Self, a woman with agency. You need to make sure you find your way to take the first step and keep going—implement, implement, implement.

Be vigilant for those moments when you want to stop making changes. Notice when and where you start to avoid or get stuck. It could be that you need to ease off, or it could be that you've met your resistance. This is where you need to reach for your self-compassion and empathy and find ways that work for you to keep going. If you stop, it could be that this isn't the change you need to make. Or you may have become disconnected from your original vision and goal.

During this phase, two things that can help you are a Support Network and a System for Keeping Your Life Organized.

## Your Support Network

Changing your life can be challenging. At times you might feel alone in the process, which is why creating a support network is essential. Include the people you live with, because any changes in your life will create changes in theirs. Who else would be a good ally? Choose people who will keep you accountable for the change you say you want to make.

Ask friends to join you in doing their own Life Design and then you can meet or check in with each other. I have different accountability groups for specific changes I'm making. Some I meet with in person; with others, I do a daily check-in using an app on my phone. Accountability can be a light touch in with others. When I reignited my qigong practice, I asked people learning the practice with me if they wanted to join an accountability group. Three of us sent a daily emoticon to our messaging group to note that we'd done the practice.

Going into nature can also help to remind you why you're making the changes and also reenergize you.

## Using a Bullet Journal

Inviting change into your life can also bring chaos. Having reliable systems to help you stay organized is essential. If you love using paper and pen, you might like the Bullet Journal method. Ryder Carroll created this method when he found his to-do lists and appointments had become scattered on sticky notes and other bits of paper. He wanted a place to put everything but didn't want to use a paper-wasting pre-printed planner. The best way to learn about the method is by seeing it. Ryder made an introduction video, which you can find online; search using his name and Bullet Journal.

Now there's a Bullet Journal movement. Thousands of people have embraced it and made innovations based on the idea. Your web search will also bring up their posts on how they've innovated or helped the method evolve. Some people create beautiful works of art; I keep mine simple, as I want to have the least time-consuming setup for organizing my life and staying on track. You can use these thought seeds to help you think well about what you want to put in place to keep your vision alive as you take action.

- What I can put in place to ensure that I will keep implementing is . . .
- What I need to put in place to keep moving forward is . . .
- Ways I will keep going with implementation are . . .
- Constructive support would look like . . .

Having worked through the ORED steps for your Life Design, and put the support in place to keep you on track, the next step is A to Act. When you take this step in a new direction for your life, to paraphrase W. H. Murray, "a whole stream of events will issue from your decision, raising in your favor all manner of unforeseen incidents and meetings and material assistance, which no [wo]man could have dreamt would have come her way."

I'm grateful you've made it this far in the book, and hopefully you have engaged with the Life Design process and have at least one Act you have committed to implementing. Now is the time to . . .

ACT

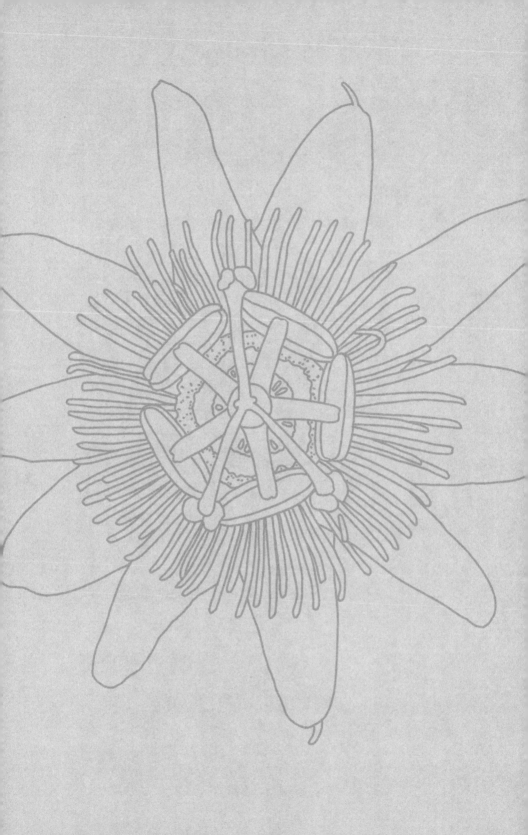

# Afterword

What's called for at this time in human history is a massive change, a change in the way we do things that may at first be inconvenient or unfamiliar. It's also well known that the only change we can really make is to change ourselves.

Living consciously as a force for positive change isn't something you're going to master by simply reading this book; however, I hope that reading it may have invoked some new thoughts for you. My deeper wish is that you engage in doing the work to unhook yourself from the ways of living that keep you defaulting to the familiar yet destructive ways of doing things.

We have weathered changes before. Possibly the most recent one we've all experienced is the rapid changes brought to our lives by the advent of the internet. These changes have taken place over 20 years and have been radical. The changes we must now make will take place in the next 10 years and must be far reaching. So yes, things are going to be unsettling, but if you engage with this process, you will be moving with the change rather than being buffeted about by it.

I wrote this book for you, and for all the beings we share this planet with. I also wrote it for myself. There are domains where I still struggle and know I need to peel off more layers. There are domains where I think, *Haven't I done enough with this? Can't I move on?* It is clear that there is more I need to do to recover my life force so that I can participate effectively in the work we need to do together. There are places in my life where I notice a disconnect between what I think I value and my actions, so I'm going to continue cleaning up my act, gently and with self-compassion.

This in depth excavation using the Life Design process need only occur once every five to seven years. Every 12 months, you can check in by reflecting on the past year, and map your next action steps.

Once you've done the work of getting your life to a place where you have more spaciousness, and you've recovered more of your personal energy, the next step is to embrace working with other people. I believe that the solutions for our collective future lie firmly in the domain of Community. The preparation work of Life Design will go a long way to supporting you when you enter this territory.

Choosing consciously to change your life in service of all life on the planet is a powerful and essential act. This choice is the beginning of how you contribute to our thriving collective future. Becoming your Sovereign Self is not an easy path, but the expanded sense of wealth you will experience by embarking on this journey will bring a more profound sense of meaning and purpose to your life and give you an anchor point as you continue navigating life through these turbulent times.

You are not alone in this journey. There are thousands of women like us all over the planet responding to the call to step more fully into our power and play a role in designing a life that works for all life on Earth.

# *Resources*

# Realms and Domains

**CORE REALM**
- Nature
- Death

**WELL-BEING REALM**
- Nourish
- Embody
- Express
- Presence
- Immerse
- Play
- Create
- Adorn

**HOMESTEAD REALM**
- Home
- Stuff
- Digital
- Transport
- Land

**AFFECTION REALM**
- Family
- Friends
- Intimate Companion

**EXCHANGE REALM**
- Livelihood
- Money
- Community

# The Life Design Process

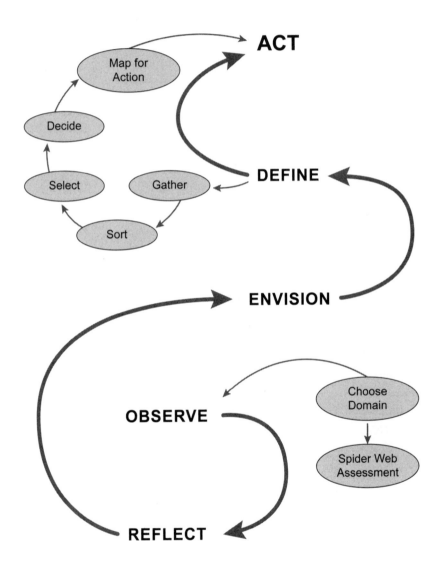

# Exercises

The following three exercises will enrich your design process. The first taps into your body's wisdom, while the second will show you the insightful source of wisdom nature can bebody, nature, and death. For the first and last exercise, you will need paper for making a drawing and writing respectively; for the second exercise, you will need to be outside in nature.

## Your Body's Wisdom Exercise

Becoming aware of your body and the sensations you feel in it can inform situations you are in. For this exercise, we are going to connect to our body's wisdom, as part of the Observe or Reflect Life Design step, and find out if there is any information that your body can provide that will support you in making your life changes. This is especially useful if you feel particularly challenged or stuck in a domain. You may want to have a friend guide you through the steps of the process, so that you don't have to break your flow to refer to the process written here.

You may already have a clear sense of which domain you want to work with. If not, pause for a moment, and look inward to sense into the domains and see which one calls your attention. Look through your journal, and find what you've written about the life-diminishing aspects of your life in this domain in the Present, in which your life force is stuck or is lost.

### Observe Your Present

How do you experience this life-diminishing aspect of your life in this present moment? Describe a specific situation recently in which you felt diminished or stuck. Describe your experience. Are there any particular things you notice, particular words, the rhythm of the experience? Did it have a temperature or an atmosphere? Make a drawing of your impressions of this life-diminishing situation, with the aim of capturing the quality of the situation through mark-making, rather than making a pretty picture.

### Reflect on Your Past

Where did this life-diminishing experience begin? Are there any people from your past that remind you of it or who you associate with it? If you have someone guiding you through the process, talk with him or her a little about the experience in order to bring it to life. Once you feel the experience more fully, find a motion or gesture that expresses the life-diminishing behavior. Maybe there are words.

Allow your body to express this gesture through repetition until you really feel it in your body. Place an object on the floor to represent this person from the past—it can be anything: a cushion, the TV remote, or your journal, for example. Then move to a different part of the room.

### Envision Your Sovereign Self (Future)

In this new place in the room, describe who you would be if you were free of this life-diminishing behavior. Describe your experience. Express it. How would you stand, and move, and dance? What sounds would you make? Really feel that self, free from the life-diminishing behavior.

Once you feel your Sovereign Self fully in your body, begin to relate with the object representing the past. Move around and toward it until you find a distance that feels comfortable. From where you are, what would your Sovereign Self do or say to this life-diminishing person? Express yourself with a posture, gesture, or movement. Amplify it until you feel the fullness of its power in your body; maybe there are words that come. Stay out of your head; let your body do the work. Gradually let the words die away, and continue with the gesture.

Slowly, let go of the movement, and in the stillness, integrate its power into your body. How can this power support you in keeping you free from the life-diminishing, stuck place? Make a note in your journal to remind you of the gesture and the power you tapped into, and to use it when you feel the need.

Thank your body for sharing its wisdom.

I adapted this exercise from one I learned from Process Oriented Psychotherapy trainer Ana Rhodes during a leadership and facilitation training. I found it to be a particularly powerful process that had beneficial ripple effects in my life after going through it, so I wanted to share it with you.

## Nature's Wisdom Exercise

You may want to gain a different perspective on the beliefs you have in a particular domain. Nature can be a great ally in imparting a perspective you may have not perceived. Select the domain you want to work with and the particular life-diminishing aspects you wrote about when you were doing your Observe and Reflect process.

Take yourself outdoors into nature. Go somewhere where you can put your feet on the earth and where you can see trees, flowers, or bushes. It could be your garden or a park. Choose a place where you feel comfortable and will be undisturbed. Have your journal nearby so that you can harvest your insights at the end of the process. You may want to invite a friend to be your guide through the process.

Once you are settled in your nature setting, bring to mind the domain you want to work with and the belief or life-diminishing aspects you wrote about. If you have a guide, briefly talk with them about this belief or life-diminishing aspect, enough for you to get a sense of it. Then let go of the talking.

Staying connected to that life-diminishing aspect, stand in a relaxed manner, with feet shoulder width apart and knees slightly bent. Let your arms hang by your sides, and lower your gaze. Connect with your breath, and inhale and exhale a few times, then take a deeper breath, and let it out. Consciously open all your senses. Raise your gaze, and open yourself to connect and receive. It may come through any of your senses. When you become aware of it, observe. What strikes you about it? What is the outstanding feature that caught your attention—its shape, its sound, its smell? Become curious about it. Notice what's going on. Begin to describe to yourself, or out loud if you have a guide, what it is you are experiencing.

Be light with this moment, notice what flirts with you. It might be the pattern in the leaves, the quality of the wind on your skin, or the scent of the forest.

Now bring to mind the life-diminishing aspects you want to work with.

How does what you've experienced inform this life-diminishing situation or aspect of your life? What insight does nature have to give you? Describe the insight either to your guide or in your journal.

How could you use this insight to support you in becoming more of your Sovereign Self?

Once you have harvested this insight, in whatever way occurs to you, thank nature for sharing its wisdom with you.

## Gathering Insight from Death

We never know when we are going to die, and most of us hope that we will live a long life. For this exercise, with pen and paper in hand, find a place where you won't be disturbed for up to an hour. You are going to put yourself in an "as if" situation, this is a useful way to surface insights. In this case, the invitation is for you to place yourself in the future at the moment your death is nearing. From this place, write a letter as if you are facing your last hours alive.

Write to a loved one, tell them what you are grateful for, write about the highlights of your life, write about challenges where you learned, and gathered wisdom from your experience. Write without stopping or censoring yourself; this is not about writing the perfect letter. Write rapidly, spelling mistakes and all. This way, you minimize the opportunity for your logical, rational mind to censor you.

The exercise is about clearing your heart of all those things that have gone unacknowledged or unsaid. Or maybe they were acknowledged or said, but they need a little more attention. From this place, you open the possibility of discovering what matters to you right now at this moment.

When you notice that you are gazing into the middle distance or thinking in more detail about that memory, gently bring yourself back to the pen and the paper and get writing again.

The simple act of writing this letter is powerful in itself. Once you've written all that you want to write, you can stop there without reading it. Or you can read it, noticing anything that surprises you or is new material. Perhaps in reading it, you will gather insight that might inform your approach to life, or what might be a new direction for exploration. You can keep the letter for a time if it's helpful, but try not to hang on to it forever. Let it go in a few months.

I first did this exercise in a forest in Mexico. It was a beautiful and powerful setting to write my death letter. As I sat with my back to a tall pine tree, I was aware of the wind gently swaying me through the tree, soothing me as I wrote—as if in a few hours I was going to die. This exercise was part of the process facilitated by my friend and colleague, Manolo Cetina, that lead to me decide to make labyrinths in New York City. In writing this letter, you have the potential to regenerate yourself, as well as discovering priorities for action.

# Bibliography

## PART 1: IN THE BEGINNING

Capra, Fritjof and Pier Luigi Luisi. *The Systems View of Life*. Cambridge: Cambridge University Press, 2014.

Hawken, Paul. *Drawdown: The Most Comprehensive Plan Ever Proposed to Reverse Global Warming*. London: Penguin, 2018.

Macy, Joanna, and Molly Young Brown. *Coming Back to Life: The Updated Guide to the Work that Reconnects*. Gabriola Island, BC: New Society, 2014.

Raworth, Kate. *Doughnut Economics*. London: Random House Business/Cornerstone, 2017.

Regeneration International. Accessed May 14, 2019. https://regenerationinternational.org.

Rippon, Gina. *The Gendered Brain: The New Neuroscience that Shatters the Myth of the Female Brain*. London: Bodley Head, 2019.

Rockström, Johan. *"Let the Environment Guide Our Development."* Filmed July 2010 at TEDGlobal. Video, 18:04. https://www.ted.com/talks/johan_rockstrom_let_the_environment_guide_our_development.

Roland, E., and G. Landua. *Regenerative Enterprise: Optimizing for Multi-Capital Abundance*. New York: Regenerative Enterprise Institute, 2013.

United Nations. *"Transforming Our World: the 2030 Agenda for Sustainable Development."* Accessed May 14, 2019. https://sustainabledevelopment.un.org/post2015/transformingourworld.

## PART 3: LIFE DESIGN: DIVING INTO YOUR DOMAINS
### Core

Duncan-Rogers, Jane. *Before I Go: The Essential Guide to Creating a Good End of Life Plan*. Rochester, VT: Findhorn Press, 2018.

Earth Protectors. Accessed May 14, 2019. https://www.stopecocide.earth.

Ecosystem Restoration Camps. Accessed May 14, 2019. https://www.ecosystemrestorationcamps.org.

Gooley, Tristan. *The Walker's Guide to Outdoor Clues and Signs*. London: Sceptre, 2015.

Mikanowski, Jacob. "A Different Dimension of Loss." Accessed May 14, 2019. https://eowilsonfoundation.org/a-different-dimension-of-loss.

Roszak, Theodore. *Ecopsychology: Restoring the Earth, Healing the Mind*. Berkeley: Counterpoint, 1995.

Wall Kimmerer, Robin. *Braiding Sweetgrass: Indigenous Wisdom, Scientific Knowledge and the Teachings of Plants*. Minneapolis, MN: Milkweed Editions, 2015.

Wohlleben, Peter. *The Hidden Life of Trees: What They Feel, How They Communicate – Discoveries from a Secret World*. Vancouver, BC: Greystone Books, 2016.

**Well-Being**

Atlas of Emotions. Accessed May 14, 2019. www.atlasofemotions.org.

Berceli, Dr. David, PH.D. "Full version: Stress, Tension, & Trauma Release 26." TRE™ Stories and Testimonials Video 12:53. https://vimeo.com/13037211.

Ekman, Paul. *Emotions Revealed: Understanding Faces and Feelings*. London: Orion Publishing Co, 2004.

Enright, Lynn. *Vagina: A Re-education*. London: Allen & Unwin, 2019.

Fair Wear Foundation. Accessed May 14, 2019. www.fairwear.org.

Good On You. Accessed May 14, 2019. www.goodonyou.eco.

Gunders, Dana. "Wasted: How America is Losing Up to 40% of Its Food from Farm to Fork to Landfill." Accessed May 14, 2019. https://www.nrdc.org/resources/wasted-how-america-losing-40-percent-its-food-farm-fork-landfill.

Jay-Lewin, Deborah. "Restoring Health and Wisdom Through Embodied Movement." TEDxFindhornSalon. Published December 4, 2017. Accessed May 14, 2019. https://www.youtube.com/watch?v=1TE2ttc5vTY.

Johnstone, Chris. *Seven Ways to Build Resilience: Strengthening Your Ability to Deal with Difficult Times*. London: Robinson, 2019.

Kurzgesagt – In a Nutshell. "Why Meat is the Best Worst Thing in the World." Published September 30, 2018. Accessed May 14, 2019. https://www.youtube.com/watch?v=NxvQPzrg2Wg.

Pitchford, Paul. *Healing With Whole Foods: Asian Traditions and Modern Nutrition*. 3rd revised edition. Berkeley, CA: North Atlantic Books, 2002.

Re-evaluation Counseling. Accessed May 14, 2019. https://www.rc.org.

The Environmental Working Group. "Skin Deep." Accessed May 14, 2019. www.ewg.org/skindeep.

The Ethical Consumer. Accessed May 14, 2019. https://www.ethicalconsumer.org.

*The Lancet Planetary Health*. "More Than a Diet." Published February 1, 2019. Accessed May 14, 2019. https://www.thelancet.com/journals/lanplh/article/PIIS2542-5196(19)30023-3/fulltext.

Weed, Susan S. *New Menopausal Years: The Wise Woman Way*. Woodstock, NY: Ash Tree Publishing, 2002.

**Homestead**

Crawford, Martin. *Creating a Forest Garden: Working with Nature to Grow Edible Crops*. Cambridge: UIT Cambridge Ltd, 2010.

Global Footprint Network. "Ecological Footprint Calculator." Accessed May 14, 2019. http://www.footprintcalculator.org.

Holistic Management International. Accessed May 14, 2019. www.holisticmanagement.org.

Ingham, E., A. R. Moldenke, and C. A. Edwards. *The Soil Biology Primer*. Ankeny, IA: Soil and Water Conservation Society, 2010.

Jacke, D., and E. Toensmeier. *Edible Forest Gardens Vol. II: Design and Practice for Temperate-Climate Permaculture*. White River Junction, VT: Chelsea Green Publishing, 2005.

Kondo, Marie. *Spark Joy: An Illustrated Guide to the Japanese Art of Tidying*. Berkeley, CA: Ten Speed Press, 2014.

Newport, Cal. *Digital Minimalism: On Living Better with Less Technology*. London: Portfolio Penguin, 2019.

Soil Food Web. Accessed May 14, 2019. https://www.soilfoodweb.com/

Weed, Susun S. *Healing Wise: The Wise Woman Herbal*. Woodstock, NY: Ash Tree Publishing, 1990.

## Affection

Gottman, John. *The Seven Principles for Making Marriage Work*. London: Orion Spring, 2018.

Perry, Philippa. *The Book You Wish Your Parents Had Read (and Your Children Will Be Glad That You Did)*. London: Penguin Life, 2019.

Wolynn, Mark. *It Didn't Start With You: How Inherited Family Trauma Shapes Who We Are and How to End the Cycle*. London: Penguin Books, 2017.

## Exchange

Ethical Markets Media. Accessed May 14, 2019. http://www.ethicalmarkets.com.

Gaia University. *Regenerative Livelihoods by Design*. Accessed May 14, 2019. https://gaiauniversity.org/rld/

Sandford, Carol. *The Regenerative Business: Redesign Work, Cultivate Human Potential, Achieve Extraordinary Outcomes*. London: Nicholas Brealey Publishing, 2017.

Brown, Brené. *Dare to Lead: Brave Work. Tough Conversations. Whole Hearts.* London: Penguin Random House, 2018.

McIntosh, Alastair. *Soil and Soul: People versus Corporate Power*. London: Aurum Press, 2004.

## Keeping the Vision Alive

Carroll, Ryder. "Bullet Journal method." Accessed May 14, 2019. www.bulletjournal.com.

Pressfield, Steven. *The War of Art: Break Through the Blocks and Win Your Inner Creative Battles*. New York: Black Irish Books, 2002.

_____. *Do the Work: Overcome Resistance and Get Out Your Own Way*. North Egremont, MA: Black Irish Books, 2011.

## Illustration Credits

All illustrations are by Ariane Burgess (line drawings) and Eddy Coodee (word clouds), with the exception of:

p. 23: Planetary Boundaries Model (Rockström and Steffen) by J. Lokrantz/Azote based on Steffen et al. 2015, www.stockholmresilience.org

p. 24: Doughnut Economics Model (Raworth) by Kate Raworth and Christian Guthier, *The Lancet Planetary Health*, https://commons.wikimedia.org/wiki/File:Doughnut_(economic_model).jpg#filelinks

p. 95: Cynefin Model (Snowden) adapted from the illustration Cynefin as of 1st June 2014 by Dave Snowden, https://commons.wikimedia.org/wiki/File:Cynefin_as_of_1st_June_2014.png

# Acknowledgments

When and where does a book begin? The seeds for this one began many years ago in nature, and the theme has been informed and influenced by people and experiences over my lifetime.

This book wouldn't exist without my experiences with a happy band of people who so willingly engaged in freeing themselves from life-limiting practices through nature connection practices.

Supported from afar by Manolo Cetina, once a month I deepened into myself in a stunning natural setting with Judith Canepa, Elizabeth Soychak, Haideen Anderson, Michael Stone, Monique Leibovitch, Jeanette Pfeiffer, Joan Beard, Aresh Javadi, Trish Doherty, and Grace Clearsen. We worked together for 18 life-changing months, relating with the earth, wind, fire, water and trees. Through these experiences each of us in our own way has gone on to work as a force for positive change. It was an honor to learn and grow with them.

I was able to call this group together because I was fortunate that my father M. Steve Burgess encouraged me to question everything. He signposted possible places to explore by instilling in me a love of reading nonfiction books full of worldview–challenging ideas. Through my explorations I realized that deep work with nature was an essential experience for navigating what he often called the "turbulent environment" we are currently living in.

Through the role-modeling of my mother, Sian Mackay, who evolved her life from a young woman who married at 19 to journalist, publisher, and author of nonfiction and fiction, I knew that writing a book was challenging yet possible.

In 2008 I entered into two life-changing, life-long learning pathways that contributed to my taking steps toward writing this book. The first was participating in the CTI Leadership training, where I was fortunate to be "called forth" by Henry Kimsey-House and Sam House. The second was to embark on my Master's degree with Gaia University, where founders

Andrew Langford and Liora Adler introduced me to good regenerative design thinking practice. Working with these four elders convinced me of the need for more people versed in leadership skills and good design thinking and who are prepared to work in the turbulent and emergent environment we are currently living in.

Specifically for the process of actually putting the ideas for this book into a form you could read, I am deeply grateful to Sabine Weeke of Findhorn Press for seeing the potential and timeliness of this book when I thought we were having a light-hearted chat. My appreciation goes to Nicky Leach, who I had the fortune to have as my insightful, patient, and encouraging editor, and Damian Keenan, who poured his design skills into the interior of the book.

My dear intimate companion, Eddy Coodee, encouraged me throughout the process, methodically proofread the text, and used his meticulous design skills to create the word clouds. During my sequestered writing time, I am thankful for the conversations and karaoke moments with Tineke Langedijk and Inger Hosbund. They enthusiastically engaged in reflections on their life domains, which in turn nourished my writing process. I'm also grateful to friend and fellow author Chris Johnstone who, from the moment we met, encouraged my writing of this book.

# About the Author

Photo by Eddy Coodee

As a regenerative designer, Ariane Burgess works with groups and individuals to design and implement life-affirming projects and communities. Her work includes Camino de Paz Labyrinths, a five-year project making labyrinths with community groups in the South Bronx, New York; the Climate Change Labyrinth with students from PS99, Queens, New York; a Zero-Waste initiative with The Park Ecovillage; and the Findhorn Food Forest in Scotland.

She passionately facilitates learning spaces where people can collaborate and develop their knowledge and skills for whole-living-systems design, which includes regenerative aspects of ecological, economic, and social design. Along with her freelance design and coaching work, she works with Gaia University, Gaia Education, and Findhorn College and offers online courses through her website **arianeburgess.com**.

Since returning to live in Scotland after 20 years in New York City, as part of her acts for positive change, she is an active member of the Scottish Green Party. She lives in Scotland with her partner, Eddy Coodee, where together they enjoy tending their homestead and taking rambling walks in the stunningly beautiful landscape.

## *Permaculture: A Spiritual Approach*
### by Craig Gibsone & Jan Martin Bang

PERMACULTURE LOOKS FOR PATTERNS embedded in our natural world as inspiration for designing solutions. It is a philosophical, spiritual, and practical approach to the use of land, integrating microclimate, functional plants, animals, soils, water management, and human needs into an intricately connected, highly productive system.

ISBN 978-1-84409-657-2

Also of Interest from Findhorn Press

## Earth Spirit Dreaming
### by Elizabeth E. Meacham

A PRACTICAL MANUAL of shamanic ecotherapy practices that help resolving the growing disconnection from nature. The Earth Spirit Dreaming process offers experiential exercises to foster interactions with the intelligences and energies of nature and the Spirit realm, calling forth a rebirth of our shamanic abilities.

ISBN 978-1-62055-987-1

FINDHORN PRESS

*Life-Changing Books*

Learn more about us and our books at
*www.findhornpress.com*

For information on the Findhorn Foundation:
*www.findhorn.org*